UNFORTUNATE SONS

UNFORTUNATE SONS

A True Story of Young Men and War

L. D. James

CAMBRIDGE DENT
PUBLISHERS

UNFORTUNATE SONS:
A True Story of Young Men and War

Copyright 2005 © Larry D. James.

Printed in the United States of America.
No part of this book may be used or reproduced
in any manner whatsoever without written
permission except in the case of brief quotations
embodied in critical articles or reviews.

For information, address
Cambridge Dent Publishers
3028 Dent Place NW
Washington, DC 20007

books@cambridgedent.com

Design by Noam Fridman

Library of Congress Control Number:
2005926193

James, Larry D.
Unfortunate Sons:
a true story of young men and war/
L.D. James
p. cm.

ISBN 0-9768619-2-5

First Edition: October 2005

*For the men of Charlie Company, Fourth Battalion,
Ninth Infantry Regiment, Twenty-fifth Infantry
Division and those who died with them in
the Hoc Mon district of the Republic of Vietnam
on March 2, 1968, and for their families.*

Contents

War is delightful to those who have no experience of it.

Desiderius Erasmus, 15th Century Dutch Humanist

Acknowledgments

It could be said that I began to write this book on the day in May of 1968 when I was assigned to the Twenty-fifth Infantry Division. I was a twenty-two-year-old first lieutenant about to take on the most difficult job of my life. I had never heard of the unit I was being sent to, the Fourth Battalion, Ninth Infantry Regiment (Manchu), and knew nothing of their recent history. The clerk at division headquarters who assigned me to them very definitely did. After instructing me where to go to catch the flight to the Manchu base camp in Tay Ninh, he looked up briefly and said, "Sorry 'bout that."

The Manchus needed replacements. It had been a difficult spring. In the preceding five months alone, the battalion losses had been enormous: 140 dead and more than 730 wounded. The record shows that until March of that year, the Manchus' experiences had been pretty much like that of other infantry units assigned to III Corps, that part of South Vietnam running from the coast through Saigon and up to Tay Ninh and the Cambodian border. But it was what happened to Charlie Company of the Manchus on March 2, 1968 that made them different. Their ambush that day cast a very long shadow, one that hung over my entire period of service with the battalion.

Throughout the Vietnam War any infantry soldier had a special place in the military hierarchy that was not related to rank. In the major base camps throughout South Vietnam the infantry soldier was not a common sight. The base camps were home to many of the support personnel, the "clerks and jerks," as the infantryman would call them. On those rare occasions when a "grunt" from the field found himself in these rear areas, he had an aura about him, a very definite look. And it was not just the ragged and faded fatigues or the scuffed, worn boots. He was different. His life was different, and it showed. He was considered a breed apart because of it. But even among the regular infantry, following the March 2, 1968 ambush, the Manchus became a special case. For a time they were considered the bad-luck battalion and grunts from other units kept their distance. It was a feeling I had almost from the first day and I was not the only one.

This account of what happened that day could not have been written without the help of many people. None contributed more than those who survived the ambush and were willing to relive those difficult hours in personal interviews and written correspondence over the space of several years. It was not an easy task for them, resurrecting the memories of an awful day in their lives. But they wanted the story to be told. So in long interview sessions they walked down that terrible road again and remembered it all—the heat, the sounds, the smells, all of it. The moments I spent with them in quiet hotel rooms and around kitchen tables as they told me their stories, are moments I treasure. The strength they displayed as they looked back inside themselves to that private place where the events of March 2 are kept deserves further examination and warrants a book of its own to do it justice.

I am especially grateful to Wayne Holloway, Dan McKinney, Denny Dubendorf, Danny Luster, Andy Rodgers, Frank Tinkle, and John Henchman for their help and for sharing their accounts of the role each of them played that day. Burt Haugen, Bob Garner, Larry Ward, Larry Mitchell, Richard Tipton, Al Baker, Larry Criteser, Keith Bolstad, Don Crowley, Ed Episcopo, Bill Fitch, Willie Gin, Gerry Schooler, Willie Gore, Ron Beedy, Todd Dexter, Larry Graves, Roger Montgomery, and Tom O'Dell also contributed valuable insights into my understanding of the atmosphere that prevailed in the days and months leading up to the ambush. I am also grateful for the support of Robert "Willy" Dixson, who laid the groundwork by being the first Manchu veteran to actively search for information on the March 2nd ambush during his many visits to Vietnam after the war.

The narrative was aided immensely by the guidance, suggestions, and encouragement of Richard Stinson, Kevin Lynch, and Susan Mickelberry. Special thanks are due to Patricia Mickelberry whose editorial advice and criticisms helped me overcome the shortcomings she uncovered in the manuscript. The final version was much the better because of her influence. There would have been no final version had it not been for the good judgment, patience, and support of my wife, Sonja Pace James.

Special thanks are due for the help I received from several of the family members, in particular Verna Slane, who generously allowed me access to all the letters her son Ron wrote home while he served in Vietnam. Showing these young men as they were, getting to know them and what they experienced of life, was essential in my effort at trying to convey the impact of their deaths. Thanks, too, to Mike Williamson for introducing me to Medal of Honor recipient Nicholas Cutinha as a young boy as the two were growing up in Alva, Florida.

In Vietnam I was helped by Nguyen Ngoc Nham, Nguyen Van Phi, Trung Van Meo, Tran Thi Mui, Nguyen Hoang Phoung, Nguyen Van Het, Tran Van Nhamh, Thich Tri Anh, Huang Dao, Nguyen Van Vamh, and the family of Nguyen Dinh Vanh: his son Nguyen Dinh Thang, wife Truong Thi Kim Lien, and sister Nguyen Thi Ma.

Verna Slane told me she had wanted to know what happened to her son and how he died. She also said she was counting on me to do the right thing by her son Ron and "all those other boys," as she put it. I hope I have. There were survivors who declined to be interviewed for this book. Should they read it, I hope they will find it as it was intended: an overdue tribute to a group of young Americans who did what was asked of them and paid with their lives.

Introduction

Let every nation know, whether it means us good or ill, that we shall pay any price, bear any burden, meet any hardship ... to assure the survival and the success of liberty.

—John F. Kennedy, January 20, 1961, Inaugural Address

The men of Charlie Company of the Fourth Battalion, Ninth Infantry Regiment (Manchu), Twenty-fifth Infantry Division were typical of young Americans coming of age in the early to mid-1960s. They were entering maturity in the long shadow of their parents' generation, a generation that, to them, had done just about everything right, saving the world from Nazism in World War II and from communism in the Korean War. Having been born to men who had answered their country's call without complaint in World War II, "baby boomers" like the men of Charlie Company felt obliged to do the same should it be asked of them.

In the 1960s the United States was engaged in

a number of ambitious projects that embodied the image Americans had of themselves as a nation: a generous people willing to sacrifice for a greater good. In the early part of the decade Peace Corps volunteers, spurred on by the encouragement of their young president, John F. Kennedy, signed up by the thousands to head for some of the most destitute countries in the world, determined to bring at least the hope of a better life to the poor. Later, some would answer the call and join Lyndon Johnson's Great Society programs address similar economic and social problems at home. Thus, the 1960s generation felt it had been called on to answer some very big challenges, and it was enthusiastic to embrace the future in the spirit of President Kennedy's imperative he outlined in his inauguration on a cold January day in 1961, "Ask not what your country can do for you, but what you can do for your country."

Those young Americans, standing in the shadow of their parents, were eager to prove their worth. Most of them did not question the judgment of their elders, who believed not only that communism was the greatest threat facing the country but also that it should be confronted wherever it was to be found. A succession of U.S. presidents had held this to be the right policy. The United States had gone toe-to-toe with the Soviets and forced them to withdraw their missiles from Cuba. Now, it seemed, the newest battlefield against communism was a small country in Southeast Asia.

In the 1950s Dwight Eisenhower, who as the supreme allied commander in Europe during World War II knew perhaps better than anyone the true costs of war, thought the price of fighting communism was worth paying. In a speech at the national governor's conference in 1953, he stated, "So, when the United States votes $400 million to help that war, we are not voting for a giveaway program. We are voting for the cheapest way that we can to prevent the occurrence of something that would be of the most terrible significance for the United States of America--our security." Eisenhower's successor, John Kennedy, expressed the same sentiment in a television interview[1]: "These people who say that we ought to withdraw from Vietnam are wholly wrong, because if we withdrew from Vietnam, the Communists would control Vietnam. Pretty soon Thailand, Cambodia, Laos, Malaya would go, and all of Southeast Asia would be under the control of the Communists and under the domination of the Chinese..." So, too, did Lyndon B. Johnson in another televised speech to the American people, when he said, "If this little nation goes down the drain and can't maintain her independence, ask yourself, what's going to happen to all the other little nations?"

With each successive administration in Washington, the mission to defend that tiny Southeast Asian nation—which most Americans could not find on a map

---

1. Sept. 2, 1963 television interview by Walter Cronkite of CBS News.

and whose name most could not pronounce—evolved. Eisenhower sent money and a handful of military advisors. Kennedy went a step further, providing training and equipment to the South Vietnamese armed forces. Under Johnson, American ground troops began to take an active role in the fighting, with the marines arriving first, in 1965. By 1968 a massive army of more than half a million American men was deployed, all in service to an undeclared war with no front lines or clear objectives.

With the leadership of a generation that had embodied selflessness, sacrifice, and doing the right thing, urging America to take up the cause of defending South Vietnam against communism, many young American men believed military service was the right thing for them to do. That did not, however, mean that every young man who served was a volunteer. In the mid-1960s there was no need to enlist. The Selective Service System, a federal agency set up to provide manpower to the armed forces in times of emergency, was conducting a draft. The draft had been in existence since the end of World War II, with virtually all men aged eighteen to twenty-five required to register for military conscription. However, until the major troop build up in Vietnam, the military had been sufficiently well-staffed with volunteers, so many were never called to serve their two years of active duty in the military.[2] That was the case when the first U.S. combat troops

2. Selective Service System mission statement

arrived in Vietnam in 1965. But as the war escalated, enlistments weren't keeping up, and the need to fill the boots on the ground grew. The way to do that was through conscription.

In 1965 about 20,000 draftees were inducted into the military each month, most were conscripted into the army. By 1968, in order to meet troop strength requirements for combat duty in Vietnam, that figure had doubled. The new conscript army was largely composed of teenagers; the average age of a U.S. soldier in Vietnam was nineteen, younger than the soldiers of World War II or the Korean War.[3]

Since all young American men were subject to the draft, the conscripted army should, in theory, have been a true cross-section of American society. It wasn't. Those conscripted were mostly from the poorer classes, for whom exemptions to the draft seemed harder to come by than for their more privileged counterparts. Of the numerous exemptions from military service that Congress had written into law, student deferments were the most far-reaching, and they had a dramatic effect on the makeup of the military. Because full-time college students in academic good standing were deferred from serving, draft laws effectively enabled most upper- and middle-class men to avoid military service altogether.[4]

Therefore, young men who were not destined for

3. Paul Atwood, "Vietnam War," Microsoft® Encarta® Online Encyclopedia 2004
4. Ibid

college knew they would have to serve. They accepted this as the inevitability it was and, in many cases, just waited for the draft notice to arrive in the mail. Others enlisted, some out of a sense of duty, some out of a desire to influence what their military service would be like, since volunteers got at least a chance to ask for certain kinds of jobs; they would not necessarily get what they asked for—but they might. As the war effort in Vietnam intensified and evolved from one in which American troops primarily served to advise the South Vietnamese military to one that saw the arrival and deployment of whole combat units, draftees were almost certain to be assigned to one of the combat arms of the army: infantry, armor, or artillery. There were exceptions, of course. On occasion, a shortage of individuals with special skills would develop, and a draftee with those skills or experience would find himself in a combat support role. Not every draftee could expect to automatically be assigned to the army either. Hundreds of conscripts found themselves unexpectedly assigned to the U.S. Marine Corps when marine enlistments weren't keeping up with demands.

Any accurate reflection of the sentiments of that time, of how American boys growing up in the early 1960s saw themselves, is easily distorted when seen through the prism of the events that followed. The years of popular dissent and mass protest against the U.S. role in Vietnam were only just beginning when many of the men who would later serve with Charlie Company of the Manchus were drafted. For them, military service seemed inevitable, and they faced that reality with a mixture of emotions. Many felt anxiety about going to war, about fighting, about killing, about dying. But many of them also considered military service a responsibility. They believed in their country and its ideals. They believed that the threat of communism had to be confronted and defeated, by military force if need be, and they were willing, if not always eager, to do what Eisenhower, Kennedy and Johnson had called on them to do. By 1967, when most of the men who would fight and die with Charlie Company were just entering the service, Lyndon Johnson was in the White House formulating a policy that would send more and more troops to Vietnam. Eventually, an American army half-a-million strong would be on the ground in Vietnam, engaged in a conflict that would directly affect everyone in America.

But the plans for that eventual buildup of forces were made long before then. In February 1965 General William Westmoreland, the overall commander of American forces in Vietnam, had asked for forty-four infantry battalions to fight the war. The Fourth Battalion of the Ninth Infantry Regiment, nicknamed the Manchus, was one of them.

ONE

The Mission

The Mission of the Rifle Company: To close with the enemy by means of fire and maneuver in order to destroy or capture him, or repel his assaults by fire, close combat and counterattack.

U.S. Army Field Manual FM 7-10: The Infantry Rifle Company

The first two pieces of shrapnel hit one after the other penetrating the soles of Dan McKinney's boots and passing straight through both his feet. For an instant he felt nothing but the sharp jerk caused by the impact of the jagged pieces of metal as they struck. Then the burning began, like a hot iron pressing against the soles of his feet. Then shock. Surprise, even. He had been hit. The pain was unbelievable, but it was only his feet. It could have been worse.

Another explosion and now shrapnel tore through his legs, on the back of his right leg and the front of his left just below the knees. Like the wounds to his feet, the first sensations were of two sharp blows followed, after an instant of no feeling at all, by a fierce burning, this time in the muscles of his calves. The intensity of this new pain took everything else from his mind. The fire in his feet was nearly forgotten.

The next blast engulfed him with numbness followed by searing pain above his right ear where a red-hot piece of metal had carved a deep furrow as it skidded along his skull. Blood flowed freely from his feet, legs, and head, soaking the cloth of his shirt and pants.

McKinney jerked his right hand back, instinctively, when another piece of shrapnel drilled between the bones of his index and middle fingers. The seventh wound, a bullet this time, hit him squarely in the back with the force of a baseball bat. The soft tissue of his skin and muscle did not alter the bullet's course or slow it down much. It wasn't until it struck a rib, breaking it, and dissipating enough energy for the copper-jacketed lead nose to mushroom slightly as it burrowed into his chest cavity before coming to rest in the spongy tissue of his lung.

Medic Ron Slane was perhaps ten yards from McKinney when he saw him get hit, but in the deadly geometry of the killing zone of an ambush even ten inches can mean everything. Not one of the ninety-two men of Charlie Company now sprawled on the ground could determine with any certainty any place that was safe. Just being alive and uninjured after the firing began was powerful reason to stay put—I'm alive, unhurt, maybe they can't see me—so the few men still able to react were not inclined to move. But Slane did not have the luxury of staying put. His job was to treat the wounded, and he could see McKinney's blood forming reddish-black pools that were seeping across the asphalt road Charlie Company had been walking down when the ambush was sprung. The bleeding had to be stopped. Slane crawled toward McKinney.

Twenty yards off to the side of the road, 1st Lt. Nguyen Ngoc Nham watched the Americans dying in front of him. He looked on without emotion as the men of his company executed the ambush plan to perfection. The falling bodies did not look like people at all. More than anything, the green clumps now scattered along the black asphalt reminded Nham of banana trees that had been cut down to be collected for burning. The bodies were people, of course, but he noted that only in an abstract way.

Most important for the thirty-four-year-old officer was that his men had the upper hand, and the massive volume of fire that they were putting into the killing zone of the ambush meant the enemy could not threaten his troops. He also took pride in the fire discipline his young soldiers showed, how they shot only at good targets, without wasting ammunition. He watched with satisfaction at the accuracy with which they cut down his enemy. It was almost more than he had hoped for. They had caught a large American force out in the open and were efficiently destroying it. The Americans were in disarray, caught so completely by surprise that they could not mount an effective defense against the withering fire of his men. The thirty men of Nham's company, one of six companies simultaneously firing on the Americans, needed no instructions from him, or help. The former marksmanship instructor did not even take his K-52 pistol out of its holster.

Lieutenant Nham was commander of First Company, Second Go Mon Battalion of the newly formed independent regiment named Quyet Thang.[5] Quyet Thang, "determined to win," was scoring the biggest success it would have during its years in the war. Nham felt proud.

The smooth efficiency of Nham's First Company was in stark contrast to the confusion of the Americans caught in the ambush. Dan McKinney's platoon leader, 2nd Lt. James O'Laughlin, was frantic. One minute his platoon had been scurrying down the road, trying to make up for a late start and get into position to begin a sweep to find the enemy; the next minute the enemy had found them, and in the worst possible way—out in the open with no cover. His platoon was caught in the killing zone of an ambush. In seconds there were men down everywhere. Some dove to the asphalt. Others simply dropped, awkwardly, dead before they hit the ground. Those still able were returning fire, shooting blindly in every direction, wherever they guessed the enemy might be. All O'Laughlin's training, all his

5. The Quyet Thang Regiment was formed in February, 1968 as part of the reorganization made necessary following the heavy Viet Cong losses suffered in the Tet Offensive.

instincts told him to get his men up and moving.

Bursts of automatic rifle fire mixed with the steady *chuk* of machine guns in a deafening roar, like some great machine chewing up everything in its path. O'Laughlin suspected there were at least two machine guns and God knew how many automatic rifles tearing into his men as they lay exposed on the surface of highway 248. In fact, more than 200 weapons— mostly automatic rifles but also several machine guns—were delivering accurate fire on the ninety-two men of Charlie Company. Given the extent of the firepower massed against them, their only chance for survival, individually and as a group, was to get out of the killing zone.

Seconds after the initial shock had registered, the twenty-one-year-old lieutenant fought against his own instinct for self preservation and got to his feet. Ignoring the snap of the bullets, gesticulating wildly, he screamed over the roar of gunfire, "Get up, move, move, assault right!" It seemed to his men that O'Laughlin wanted them to assault a tree line nearly 100 yards away across open rice paddies. They were all out in the open with no cover. There were no trees, no ditches along the roadway, no nearby rice-paddy dikes to get behind, no protection of any kind from the guns that seemed to be in the trees on the other side of those rice paddies. To run forward along the road would be to run directly into a machine gun. It seemed equally foolish to turn back the way they had come and try to run a gauntlet of 400 yards while the Viet Cong fired from all sides—assaulting right, across that huge expanse of empty rice paddies toward the tree line where the enemy just had to be seemed like the very worst option.

It was impossible.

So they did nothing.

To O'Laughlin his men had no other option but to assault toward the tree line, somehow move past the ambushers, and get out of the killing zone. There was no way of knowing if any of his men would make it, but they had to try. If they stayed where they were, it was certain they all would die.

The sequence of events that led O'Laughlin, McKinney, Slane, and the eighty-nine other men of Charlie Company to be on that road on that hot and sunny March day had begun about a month earlier.

On January 31, 1968 the regular forces of Hanoi's Peoples Army of Viet Nam (PAVN) joined with thousands of guerrillas from the People's Liberation Armed Forces (Viet Cong) to launch an all-out, massive, coordinated attack across the Republic of Vietnam. The campaign involved some 80,000 PAVN and Viet Cong troops, and was timed to coincide with the nationwide Vietnamese holiday of Tet, the lunar New Year. A truce was in effect at the time, and although U.S. military intelligence suspected an attack was possible, the offensive came as a huge surprise.

No one was more surprised than the American public, which had been told that the massive buildup that had nearly 500,000 Americans on the ground in Vietnam was having the desired effect and that America was winning the war and putting down the communist insurgency. But the images of Viet Cong guerrillas lying dead on the grounds of the American embassy in Saigon, after having actually controlled an area inside the compound for six hours,[6] caused many Americans to start questioning what the White House and the Pentagon had been telling them. With this once elusive enemy seeming suddenly to be everywhere and in big numbers, the war that America's leaders had been telling them was so well in hand certainly didn't look that way.

Still, after the initial shock caused by the suddenness and intensity of the attacks had worn off, U.S. forces quickly gained the upper hand, their superior numbers and uncontested supremacy in the skies of South Vietnam enabling them to deal heavy losses to PAVN and Viet Cong forces. Within a few weeks, the level of fighting had returned to pre-Tet levels in most places. Most places, but not all.

One source of continuing trouble, perhaps more from a public-relations perspective than from a military one, was the ongoing resistance around Saigon. Of particular concern were the almost daily rocket attacks on Tan Son Nhut airbase on the northern outskirts of the South Vietnamese capital. The attacks were

6. Nineteen Viet Cong guerrillas attacked the U.S. Embassy at 0300, killed two U.S. military police, and held off a helicopter assault by U.S. paratroops until daylight. The embassy was not secured until 0900 the morning of February 1, 1968.

threatening air operations at the base to be sure, but more important, they were in plain view of American journalists based in Saigon. The regular, if mostly inaccurate, rocket attacks served as a constant reminder to those journalists, and thus to the American public, that the enemy remained a threat.

As part of the effort to end the attacks, U.S. troops were deployed at what seemed to be their source, a district just north of Saigon known by the name of its largest village, Hoc Mon.

TWO

The Place

Never let the enemy pick the battle site.

—General George S. Patton

The Saigon River is the lifeblood of south-central Vietnam. Its headwaters are near the Cambodian border where they form a natural boundary between Tay Ninh, Binh Phuoc and Binh Duong provinces. The river flows some 280 kilometers from the hills of Loc Ninh in Binh Phuoc province southwest to Tan Thuan, where it is joined by the Dong Nai River before emptying into the South China Sea. By the time it reaches the city of Saigon the river has become a broad expanse of muddy brown water, and it is near enough to the sea to be affected by the ebb and flow of the tides. This characteristic has been used to good advantage for thousands of years by the Vietnamese, who built an intricate network of canals in the Hoc Mon District.

During that part of the year when their rice crops needed plenty of water, farmers cut open the earthen dikes that surrounded the paddies and let the rising tide flood the fields. Before the water receded they simply plugged the hole again with mud. (A simple solution to one of the many irrigation problems faced by rice farmers elsewhere in Vietnam, who did not benefit from the natural lifting phenomenon of the tides and thus had to employ more elaborate mechanical systems of pumps and water wheels.) The canals in Hoc Mon, which had been dug and dredged over centuries, also streamlined the effort of getting crops to market; the harvest could be loaded on sampans and simply floated downstream. And for a small, mobile guerrilla force, the dozens of canals in the Hoc Mon area made it easy to come and go as they pleased, especially given the excellent concealment offered by the dense foliage along the canal banks and nearby swampy areas.

But the same characteristics that proved so useful to the Viet Cong insurgents presented significant challenges to conventional-army operations, especially operations involving the large forces typical of those the U.S. Army had deployed in Vietnam. Hoc Mon's environment is very wet, nearly always very muddy, and parts of it become inaccessible when the incoming tide floods wide areas to a depth of six feet or more. At low tide the canal bottoms are little more than swampy bogs of waist-deep mud. At high tide fording the streams is difficult, and men loaded down with weapons and other heavy equipment cannot be expected to wade or swim from one bank to another. Using the bridges on the main roadways is also problematic, since bridges act as choke points, constricting the movement of troops by forcing them to follow a predictable path. Only if special efforts are made to secure the bridges can they be used with any degree of safety.

The job of finding and destroying the enemy forces operating in this difficult terrain around Hoc Mon fell to the Manchus, the Fourth Battalion, Ninth Infantry Regiment of the Twenty-fifth Infantry Division. The unit had arrived in Vietnam on April 29, 1966 aboard the *USNS General Nelson M. Walker*, when the Twenty-fifth Division (Tropic Lightning) was sent over from its base in Hawaii during the first major wave of the U.S. troop buildup. The Manchus had seen action from the beginning. Even the advance party sent to prepare the way for the battalion lost a man a full two weeks before the main body arrived.

Until the Tet offensive of 1968, most Manchu operations had been confined to the South Vietnamese provinces near the Twenty-fifth Division's three main base camps in Cu Chi, Tay Ninh and Dau Tieng. Their new orders took them to an unfamiliar area in Gia Dinh province on the very outskirts of Saigon. In the months immediately before their deployment in Hoc Mon, the Manchus had been operating in War Zone C, a major Viet Cong stronghold that had been a sanctuary for insurgents for more than twenty years. A place with no civilians, no roads, and no large open areas, War Zone C was classified by the U.S. military as a free-fire zone, meaning that anyone encountered in that area was considered an enemy and could be engaged with deadly force without question. In War Zone C, each company in the battalion, for the most part, operated independently, with all four working together only occasionally. Each company, usually at a strength of somewhere between ninety and one hundred men, was regularly airlifted into a remote jungle clearing where it would begin a sweep, searching for enemy base camps.

When one of the battalion's companies encountered the enemy—which happened frequently, though not daily—a firefight would ensue. Since the Viet Cong and regular North Vietnamese Army forces in War Zone C did not typically emerge to fight during daylight hours, the numerous firefights were almost always the result of a Manchu company running into an enemy base camp. Each company moved during the day, routinely avoiding trails or open areas. Since visibility in the jungle was limited to a few feet, walking single file was a necessity, and flank security was impossible; anyone sent alone into the jungle would almost certainly be cut off or lost before he had gone more than a few steps. At night, each company either concealed its position or built a strong, heavily fortified one that was able to withstand an enemy assault.

The move to the Hoc Mon area meant dramatic changes. There were civilians there, and it was nearly impossible to tell noncombatants from the enemy. Roads and trails were numerous and hard to avoid. The large, wide-open rice paddies covered acres and acres of real estate, thus ruling out concealment of troop movements. Different security arrangements had to be made. To detect potential ambushes, men had to be sent ahead and to the sides of the company formation, anywhere an enemy force might be hiding in wait. New terrain, new tactics. The officers and men of the Manchus faced a completely different type of war than they had been fighting over the past few months.

The young men who made up the Manchus were, by 1968, mostly draftees, the sons of farmers, factory workers, shop clerks, and mechanics. They were neither draft-exempt college students nor the sons of senators, congressmen, or other powerful families who could use their influence to keep their sons out of harms way.

One of them was Ron Slane.

THREE

The Men

You could not be visited by a band of
friends half so fine as surround me here.

—Wilfred Owen, letter home, November, 1918.

Slane

It was just like Ron Slane to bring a slide rule to Vietnam. He liked the detail of things. Even in childhood, he had loved to tinker with things to see how they worked, to take them apart and put them together again. He was never content just to use an object; he wanted to know how it worked. His fascination with things electrical earned him the nickname "Sparky." Slane was a regular participant in school science fairs and 4-H projects. His inquisitive nature led him to question the way things were made and to see if perhaps the design could be improved. These traits, exhibited all his life, had resulted in a self-confident, even headstrong, young man, full of questions and not timid about asking them. But he did not just question the how and what of things; he also questioned the why. As a young man, he had embraced a religion that rejected the structure and authority of traditional Christian churches. Although the sect went by no official name, many of its adherents called it The Truth. One of the tenets of Slane's faith was that war, for any reason, is wrong. Slane held this belief very strongly. He would not kill.

He had been attending Oregon State University in Corvallis when his draft notice came. Since he was enrolled as a full-time student and his grades were good, he met all the criteria for exemption from the draft, so perhaps his draft notice was sent in error, maybe a clerical mix-up at the school registrar's office or at his local draft board in Lincoln City, Oregon. To satisfy the draft board that he qualified for student deferment, all Slane had to do was present copies of the right documents. He decided not to do it. Although opposed to war, Slane believed he had a duty to serve his country, so he volunteered for the draft as a conscientious objector and was guaranteed duty in the Medical Corps. He would try to preserve life, not take it. By the time he found himself in Hoc Mon patrolling the marshes and rice paddies, he had already spent five months in the field and had many opportunities to put that commitment to the test.

Although Slane's devotion to his religion had caused a certain tension in the family—his mother feared that his newfound spirituality was cutting him off from her and his three brothers and two sisters—it was soon put aside as the family faced the prospect of Ron heading to the army and almost certainly to Vietnam. No one in Slane's family questioned his decision to serve. Had they said so he probably wouldn't have listened to them anyway—there was that stubbornness that served him so well in his technical pursuits. Since the physical sciences appealed to him, he planned to study them when he returned to college after serving. In the meantime he would content himself by delving into medicine, something that was both an intellectual challenge and satisfied his desire to serve his country in a way that did not conflict with his religious convictions.

When he arrived at Ft. Sam Houston, Texas, Slane wasn't surprised to find there were a lot of other guys there just like him, conscientious objectors who had opted for the medical corps as a way to avoid service as a combat soldier. His months at Ft. Sam Houston—where he learned real, practical skills—were interesting to him and challenging, and he received top honors in the Basic Combat Medic Training Company. He then moved to Hunter Army Airfield just outside Savannah, Georgia, where he was assigned not to any job that seemed like an inevitable call-up to Vietnam, but to the Obstetrics and Gynecology Department of the Army Hospital, where he spent six months helping deliver babies.

Then came the levy for Vietnam with his name on it. On September 18, 1967, after an eighteen-hour flight with stops in Hawaii and Okinawa, a TWA Boeing 707 with Ron Slane aboard landed at Bien Hoa Airbase outside Saigon. His assignment was with the Manchus. He was told he could expect duty that would give him a mix of service, both at the battalion aid station at the main base camp in Cu Chi, and with an infantry company in the field. Slane spent the first month at the dispensary in Cu Chi changing dressings and giving shots. In his spare time he was assigned extra duty performing maintenance on the headquarters company's jeeps and ambulances.

Ron was busy, but he was also homesick. As he went about his chores, he often found his thoughts drifting to family and friends back home in Oregon. Outsiders might think of Oregon as a cool, damp place where the sun appears only when it pleases the rain gods, but Slane knew better. His family had often hit the road in their old pickup truck and camper to explore the state beyond its rainy coastal plain. He remembered times when they had crossed the Cascades and headed for the high desert of Central Oregon, ready to pull off and spend the night wherever it struck their fancy, the windows open breathing in the fragrant balsam of the junipers.

At times, he felt he could almost smell the fresh sage and see the dew-speckled dust that swirled up in little clouds as, in his memory, he walked a rutted dirt road toward a herd of wild horses grazing on a hillside. He remembered the horses shying away as he approached, and how he had stood quietly under a tree and watched them moving nervously, snatching a bite of the coarse grass, their nostrils snorting plumes of frosty horse breath in the cold dry air. He remembered their leader, a stocky mustang with scruffy brown hair who approached him boldly, purposefully, standing between him and the herd. If Slane thought about it long enough, he could still see the mustang's ears pricked up and the soft brown eyes gazing at him.

But the temptation to dwell on such memories was to be resisted. For someone as practical as Ron Slane, there was no profit in daydreams. To fight homesickness, Ron stayed busy with his assignments at the aid station at the Manchu base camp, and maintaining the jeeps and light trucks in the battalion motor pool. His mood lifted considerably when he met Richard Shockely and Gary Bledsoe, both of whom who shared his religious beliefs. But the days in the relative comfort and safety of Cu Chi were about to end.

In late October Slane got word that he was being sent out on a re-supply helicopter to join Delta Company where he was to serve six months as a platoon medic. Almost immediately he got a taste of what he could expect. In a letter to his younger brother Steve, he wrote,

> This war has all of a sudden jumped right into my lap. . . . It's not a game anymore. A medic from D Company caught infectious hepatitis and I have to take his place. . . . So now I am a medic with "D" Company for a

while.... Tomorrow night if everything goes the way they say, we're scheduled for ambush patrol. And that is where Charlie is waiting for us. It's the real thing and I'm scared. Not of dying, though, I have faith in the promises of my God. What frightens me is will I be able to care properly for those men that I am responsible for? I've earned the name "Doc" for what little I have done for them, but will I be able to keep "up tight" when the chips are down? I think so but who knows for sure. I never realized the responsibility of my position before. But that is what makes the Big Count, no matter where you are! That, and being able to fulfill your responsibilities to your fellow man.

In his letters to his mother, Verna, however, Slane was upbeat and positive, even mundane. He would ask his mother, a photojournalist, for advice on which camera to buy or what courses to take when he returned to Oregon State University.

Ron Slane's assignment to Delta Company lasted only a few weeks before he was transferred to Bravo Company, which had found itself short of medics. He was glad for the change, finding himself more comfortable with the way Bravo Company did business. Bravo Company's commander seemed more cautious, more sensible about operations, at least relative to Delta Company's commander. But the

Bravo assignment was also short-lived, as the need for medics elsewhere meant Slane found himself shuttled to Charlie Company to fill a shortage there. His time with three out of the four rifle companies in the battalion had given him a good exposure to the overall state of things. It also set him up for a promotion to Specialist 5, equivalent to buck sergeant, and perhaps more important, it led to his transfer from a rifle platoon to the company commander's command group.

"Say Mom, I am now a senior medic for Charlie Company," Slane wrote in early November. "I'm getting fat and lazy at my new position. No more ambush patrols or night activities. I just stick close to the captain and make sure everyone gets their malaria pills until we start getting shot at. And that hasn't happened since we left Cu Chi."

But life with the company commander was no free ride either; it had its own dangers, as Ron Slane found out just days into the New Year when he was wounded in a major battle between the Manchus and a large North Vietnamese force. He broke the news to his mother as gently as possible.

> You know all the statistics of GIs wounded in Vietnam? Well, I'm a reluctant statistic, but a very minor statistic at that. Thought I'd better let you know before you found out some other way and got shook up. Really, nothing very serious. Kinda like buckshot and in the

logical place to catch it, if I had been raiding someone's melon patch. It'll be hard sitting down for a while and walking I don't relish. But I'll be back with my men in a couple of days. I didn't even plan to come in out of the field, but they decided to give me a few days rest anyway.

The tale he told his brother Steve was much more candid.

I guess I'm pretty fortunate to still be alive to write to you. I didn't dare tell Mom how close I came to being NOT—about four feet to target dead center. Don't tell her 'cause it will shake her all up. And besides, the killing radius of an 82mm mortar is 10 meters. That's better than 30 feet. By all rights me and the other two guys should be dead. I'm still picking out tiny bits of shrapnel. I tell you brother; things are getting just a bit too hairy for this young troop. I'd trade my aid bag for a one way ticket home any day of the week. Any takers? The 4th of the 9th is now involved in Operation Yellowstone and we are operating nearly on top of the Cambodian border. Have we been in the news at all?

Operation Yellowstone was a big deal for the Manchus, involving numerous clashes with large numbers of

North Vietnamese troops. In one incident, Charlie Company got caught in an ambush with heavy fire coming from both flanks. Before the company commander could assess the situation and determine where the automatic-weapons fire and rocket-propelled grenades were coming from, there were already many wounded. But the initial fury of the enemy attack was met with a sustained volume of fire from Charlie Company, and after a few minutes there was a lull.

Charlie Company then assaulted left to a tree line a dozen yards distant, trying to break the enemy hold on the left flank. The move was met with a renewed volume of fire from the North Vietnamese regulars, and as the Americans moved into the tree line, an enemy claymore mine detonated. A moment of silence followed. Then came the cry.

"Medic!"

From the relative safety of the company-command group in the rear, Slane leapt up, one hand holding his helmet on his head, the other clutching his aid bag and took off at a run toward the sound of the wounded man's voice. Rocket-propelled grenades hissed past him while automatic rifles fired repeated short bursts in his direction. Slane kept running. Having shown himself, Slane knew his only hope was to make it to the protection of the tree line twenty-five yards ahead. Slightly winded and jumping with adrenaline, he reached the trees and found protection in a small ditch where the wounded man had been hit by shrapnel from the exploding mine. The slight depression of the ditch provided protection from the enemy shooters, and Slane was able to work on the wounded man without fear of being shot himself, although he knew he would not be able to move until the enemy position was knocked out. So, for the next forty minutes, as the firefight raged, he applied pressure bandages to the worst of the fallen soldier's wounds and lay next to him reassuring him that he hadn't been hurt too badly, that he'd be okay.

That had been a close one. Slane had learned that no matter how good your company commander, bad things could still happen to the best troops. Nicholas Cutinha knew it, too.

Cutinha

Everyone called him Porky. A beefy kid, with a quick smile and mischievous nature, Specialist Fourth Class Nicholas Cutinha got to carry the "pig"—the M-60 machinegun. It was heavy, twenty-three pounds not counting ammunition. Of all the weapons carried by the infantryman, the M-60 was the most powerful, capable of putting out an initial rate of fire of 600 rounds a minute. With a maximum range of 2.3 miles, it could be used with reasonable accuracy up to 1,100 yards. Unlike the sometimes troublesome M-16 automatic rifle, the pig was fairly dependable, and few in the squad complained too much when asked to carry the 100-round belts of M-60 ammunition, though they weighed ten pounds apiece. Designed as a crew-served weapon—that is, it was operated by a machine gunner, assistant gunner, and ammo bearer—the M-60 had a removable barrel, which had to be changed after 200 to 300 rounds to prevent overheating and stoppages when used in rapid-fire mode. It could be mounted on a folding bipod, one of which was usually attached to it.

So the gun and its ammunition made for a heavy load. And Cutinha, like every other Manchu infantryman, also had other stuff to carry: at least two one-quart canteens (two pounds each), four hand grenades (one pound each); perhaps a claymore mine or two (three-and-a-half pounds each), and one or more C-ration meals (two pounds each). Even with a reasonably light load of ammunition, it was easy to pack on forty-five or fifty pounds of gear before heading out into the 90-plus degree heat for long walks that often involved slogging through knee-deep mud or heavy jungle. A certain level of fitness was mandatory. Cutinha, like any soldier, even in a regular infantry unit like the Manchus, knew that if you weren't physically fit to begin with, a few weeks humping such heavy loads through the fields and forests of South Vietnam would get you in shape. Learning how to operate in such a demanding climate was a challenge. Learning to identify with the unit was not anywhere near as difficult, especially with one with a history like the Manchus.

The Ninth Infantry Regiment, as the Manchus are properly called, dates back to its founding on July 16,

1798. It was created as part of a move by Congress to shore up the national defense as tensions with one-time ally France grew. In 1800 the regiment was disbanded, but re-formed and saw action in the War of 1812. In fact, prior to the Vietnam War, the Ninth had seen action in most U.S. wars and military actions: the Mexican War in 1847, the Civil War,[7] the Western Frontier,[8] Cuba,[9] the Philippine Insurrection, World War I, World War II, and the Korean War. But it was their service in China—the Ninth Infantry Regiment was sent as part of the American Expeditionary Force to help the British put down the Boxer Rebellion—that gave the Manchus their nickname and their trademark Manchu moustache. Eventually the U.S. Army reorganized, doing away with regiments as an organizational component but, in a nod to tradition, keeping regimental designations for the battalions. Even though most of the Manchus serving in Vietnam had never heard of the regiment before arriving in country, they soon embraced its traditions.

Like nearly everyone else in the battalion, Porky sported a Manchu moustache. Growing one was a big deal for any Manchu. It set them apart from other units

7. Murfreesboro, Chickamauga, Chattanooga, Mississippi, Tennessee, Kentucky, Georgia, and Atlanta
8. The Ninth fought some 400 skirmishes with numerous Indian tribes.
9. On July 1, 1898, the regiment crossed the San Juan River and participated in the assault and seizure of San Juan Hill with Roosevelt's Rough Riders.

that were limited to the by-the-book, regulation, trim-and-slim lines of closely cropped hair on the upper lip. The Manchu moustache was something else. It could be as big and bushy as all the hormones a nineteen- or twenty-year-old could muster. Some wore it handlebar style, waxed and curled upward at the tips; others opted for a neat and trim version that recognized, in part anyway, army regulations; most, however, chose to wear it in true Manchu style, with long, drooping ends that curled down to or beyond the jaw line. It was a little bit rebellious, a thumb in the eye of the military establishment, and yet part of the tradition of the regiment. Cutinha liked that. His Manchu moustache was, without question, the biggest, bushiest, and best in the company, if not the whole battalion.

If Nick Cutinha stood out as having the best moustache he may have been unique in another respect in that he had to be among the few Manchus who felt the Hoc Mon environment was not totally alien. All he had to do was squint a little bit and the rice paddies, canals, and pineapple patches could look just like the rivers and fields around his hometown of Alva, Florida. The Saigon River to the east and the canals of Hoc Mon could just as easily have been the Caloosahatchee River and Fighter's Creek of Lee County. It wouldn't have been all that out of the ordinary to imagine his mother's shrimp boat tied up along the bank of one of those canals. Mama Bean, as everybody called her, had been the constant in his life. The self-confidence of a woman who could command respect in the man's world of fishing for shrimp far offshore in all weather in the Gulf of Mexico was reflected in her son. So, when things got bad, all he would need to do would be to think of each day's operation as a walk through the familiar swampy areas back home, and it could seem less forbidding. And Vietnam didn't have any alligators, so he didn't have to worry about losing a leg in some reptile's jaws.

By the first of March, Cutinha was winding up his fourth month in the field with the Manchus. To the other men in First Platoon he exuded self confidence and appeared quite comfortable in the rough living conditions that life in the field brought.

No one in the whole battalion could have provided a sharper contrast to the confident and competent Cutinha than newcomer Dan McKinney.

McKinney

Dan McKinney had just arrived in country when he was flown in as a replacement for Charlie Company on February 26, a day after they had arrived in the Hoc Mon district. It was all new for the twenty-year old private, first class from the tiny farming community of Hord, Illinois, population 900, and he had no idea what to expect. From what he'd seen on the evening news before he left home, he didn't know whether he should expect to come under fire immediately when his plane landed at the huge American air base at Bien

Hoa. That didn't happen, but in every other way it was as bad as or worse than he had expected. There had been firefights and casualties every day since he had joined the company. He felt on pins and needles all the time wondering what was going to happen next. It was a tough environment to learn in. And there was a lot to learn that hadn't been taught in his scant sixteen weeks of infantry training.

As was often the case with new men coming into an infantry company in the field, McKinney was not immediately embraced by the rest of his comrades. The experience for the men of the Manchus was no different than most other American infantry soldiers. There was almost always a kind of coolness on the part of the other men toward the new guys. Whether justified or not, there was a perception that a new guy was more likely to get hurt or killed than one of the old hands, and so others avoided getting too close to the newcomer as a sort of emotional self-protection; it was easier to take the death of someone in your unit if you didn't know him well. But there had to be a mechanism, too, for dealing with the loss of those you had become friends with.

The infantrymen distancing themselves from such emotions took the form that, from an outsider's point of view anyway, may have seemed a sort of casual indifference to the violence. Whenever something bad happened, McKinney was surprised, shocked almost, to hear someone grunt "that was a mother but it don't mean nothing, not a damn thing,'" even when the man saying it had just lost a close friend. There were no outward signs of sadness or hurt. Tears weren't common either in public or private.

"Don't mean a damn thing" was the way to accept it and move on since there was absolutely nothing to be done about it. The guy who was all the time pulling out that picture of his girlfriend back home, talking about how wild it got in "Nap" town on a Saturday night, as if Indianapolis ever got wild; the guy everyone had come to rely on as just being there, was gone, and there was nothing anybody could do about that. The operations weren't going to stop. Everyone knew he had to do his year no matter what happened. There'd still be "212 days and a wake-up" before there could be any thought of getting on that plane and heading home. So they would simply load the body of their friend on the med-evac, surprised, maybe, that there wasn't an urge to cry, or mourn, or feel much of anything. The *whump, whump, whump* of the rotor blades would retreat into the night sky, and they would still be right where they were, listening to the insects buzzing in the bush. They'd kneel down in some muddy ditch, rinse their friend's blood from their hands, and the monotonous cycle of night ambush patrols and daylight sweeps, humping through the rice paddies and scrub forest with the mosquitoes, and leeches and wait-a-minute vines, would continue without interruption. It didn't mean a thing.

McKinney didn't see this behavior as the defense mechanism it was. It just seemed as though the guys around him didn't care about much of anything. It wasn't at all apparent that their behavior drew attention to just how very much the deaths really did matter. But McKinney didn't see it that way. To him these guys seemed to simply shrug off the heat, the hardship, and the deaths as though they really did mean nothing. All of it made McKinney lonely. About the only thing he could be thankful for was that he had been assigned to First Platoon as an ammo bearer for machine-gunner Nick Cutinha. It turned out that Cutinha wasn't like the rest of the guys. He was warm and welcoming and the two rapidly bonded. For a new guy it was unusual to be accepted early on, especially by a well-regarded veteran like Cutinha, and for that McKinney was grateful.

Cutinha's friendship was especially welcome to McKinney because of what was happening in the life he had left behind. He was going through quite a bit of anxiety over Linda, his new wife back in Illinois who was awaiting confirmation from the doctor of her suspicion that she was pregnant. McKinney knew he had a lot to live for and wondered how he was going to manage to make it through the next year if every day was going to be like what he had experienced so far.

Holloway

Wayne Holloway was glad to be in Charlie Company's weapons platoon. For him, wrestling with the heavy and awkward 81mm mortar tubes and the heavy ammunition they fired was certainly no fun, but it was a lot better than being a rifleman. The infantry rifle company was normally configured with three rifle platoons and a weapons platoon. The rifle platoons had the M-16s, machine guns, and grenade launchers. The weapons platoon had the mortars and recoilless rifles.

Sometimes the company would establish some sort of base of operations, either with another company, or even with all four companies of the battalion. What that meant was that the weapons-platoon soldiers tended to stay in place and not take part in the daily search-and-destroy missions, the sweeps. Neither would they be involved in ambush patrols that were sent out each night. It was the rifle platoons that made the daily sweeps and the night ambushes. Weapons platoon would stay put, ready to provide indirect fire support for the rifle platoons, any time, day or night. That suited Holloway just fine. But that was only usually the case. At times the weapons platoon became just another rifle platoon.

The mission that had brought the men to Hoc Mon meant the Manchus were constantly on the move. There would be no chance to set up mortars. Each member of weapons platoon would be just another rifleman.

In addition to this unwelcome role, Holloway had in the back of his mind the curious relationship that had developed with Leroy "Chief" Nelson. The two had met when Holloway first joined weapons platoon but really had not gotten to know each other. Chief—a nickname that the Navajo soldier from the reservation outside Flagstaff, Arizona, would have preferred not to have—was shy and a loner. Chief and Holloway had found themselves together on guard duty one night, and Holloway took the opportunity to try to get to know Chief better, draw him out of his shell. He had tried to start a conversation, but his attempts at small talk were met with stony silence. Thinking that perhaps Nelson hadn't heard him well, Holloway continued his banter, at times repeating what he had said earlier, when he was abruptly cut off.

"I don't like you," was all Nelson said. For the outgoing Holloway, that blunt comment hurt. And it started him wondering, even if just a little, "Am I hard to get along with? Does he think that because I'm a southern boy, I'm a racist? Alvin Cayson doesn't seem to think so and he's black. We get along real well."

It was just another thing in the back of Holloway's mind as he tried to find his place in Charlie Company. It would help to have some friends because some of what he was experiencing was pretty hard to understand, like the day he came across a dead Manchu. He didn't know the man, couldn't see his face, in fact. Holloway had been walking along a dike as Charlie Company moved to support another of the battalion's companies, and there he was, an American boy, laid out on his back, covered in a rubber-coated green poncho with the boots sticking out. Holloway didn't know how to react. It looked so strange, especially the boy's boots.

His eyes kept being drawn to the boots, neatly tied, the laces tucked away in the tops, the jungle-fatigue trousers neatly bloused. Why was such a simple image so disturbing? It wasn't like looking at some horrible, gruesome wound. You would expect that to be upsetting. It was just a pair of boots, the polish long worn off from the constant cycle of immersion and drying out as the soldier walked the rice paddies and canals. Maybe it was the just plain normality of it that made him wonder. Had the boy put on dry socks that morning? Some guys were really good at keeping one pair of dry socks in reserve so that after even the worst of nights lying out in the rain or submerged in some canal, there would be that singular satisfaction that only dry socks could bring. Had he been one of those guys? The boy could not have known what lay ahead as he put his boots on that morning. Had he just put his boots on as he always did, maybe even enjoying, just like Holloway, the comforting feeling of a pair of dry socks?

Holloway had to look away, but the image of the boots remained. "This is real," he thought. A few minutes later Holloway found himself walking past a dead enemy soldier. His body was hard to look at, too. Holloway began to think, "I could be killed too. Or maybe I might have to kill someone else." He wasn't sure at that moment which was worse, and he couldn't help wondering, "Do all soldiers feel this way, or is it just me?"

Dubendorf

There was only one word to describe Denny Dubendorf: confident. Just nineteen years old but a veteran of more than five months in the field, he had rapidly developed into one of the men his comrades in Second Platoon had come to rely on. He was among a select group who just naturally assumed leadership positions in the squad and the platoon despite the fact that their rank was too low, technically, to warrant the posts. Leadership came naturally to Dubendorf

It had been a short trip from the halls of Dewitt High School in Dewitt, Michigan, to the jungles of Vietnam, and one he was happy enough to make. With no real plans beyond graduation, he had been content for a while to contemplate a future built around his overriding passions for hot cars and girls. But eventually restlessness overtook those passions, and the idea of joining the army began to take root. His dad and his uncle had both fought in World War II. His grandfather had fought in World War I. Males from every generation of the Dubendorf family had been to war, going back as far as the Civil War. Nothing had more appeal than to be a soldier, and not just any soldier. He wanted to be special, join some elite group. Airborne infantry was what he wanted, and he wanted to see combat, too, to prove himself. A war seven-thousand miles away in a tiny country he'd never heard of seemed like just what he needed. Come home a hero and he wouldn't be able to keep the girls off him with a stick. The army recruiter said he could help make those dreams come true.

So as enlistment time approached he felt ready. There he was, about to embark on what most of those around him saw as a potentially life-threatening experience, yet it was no big deal for him. Sure it would mean some changes but nothing he couldn't handle, and besides it might be exciting, especially the thought of going to jump school. Dubendorf could see himself all decked out in the dress green uniform, spit-shined black jump boots, airborne patch on his cap. He'd look good. He could just see himself home on leave, cruising through town on a Friday night, the exhaust note of his jet black '65 Chevy Super Sport singing its throaty song as he cruised down the main drag in Dewitt. The muscular rumble of the engine with its high-performance cam was always cool, but to be able to top it all off by being outfitted in his airborne rig, well, that would be something. That would make an impression on the girls, as if he needed any help in that department. It might be alright, a couple of years in the army. If he didn't like it, then he'd just go in, do his time, and come home to the cars and the girls and the only world he really knew or cared about. What was real was what seemed like a world of possibilities stretching out ahead of him, as limitless as the distant horizon.

Even the roughness of basic training in Fort Knox, Kentucky, couldn't change his mind. But then came advanced infantry training at Fort Gordon, Georgia, and the dream started to unravel. The army had decided that a bout with polio in childhood had left Dubendorf ill-equipped to meet the physical challenges that airborne training required. Unfit for airborne school, he had to lower his expectations a peg or two. He knew he was still going to see combat in Vietnam, but when the orders came he wouldn't be striding off to meet his destiny in spit-shined black Corcoran Jump Boots as a member of some storied unit like the Screaming Eagles of the 101st Airborne Division. He would be making the trip in a wrinkled khaki shirt and pants and low quarter shoes, just like everybody else assigned as a regular, plain-old, straight-leg infantry soldier—just another ground pounder. It was the luck of the draw that sent him to the Manchus as a replacement.

Luster

Danny Luster was a "lifer," someone who had actually enlisted in the army with thoughts of a military career. Acceptance of the inevitability of being drafted, maybe even volunteering for the draft so you could go in, do your time, and go home, or maybe enlist for a short term because you thought you owed it to your country, well that was one thing. But to plan on the army as a career? That was something else again. Of course, such anti-lifer sentiments were often only formed after experiencing army life. Sixteen weeks of constant harassment and verbal abuse took quite a bit of the glamour out of what it meant to be a soldier. An eighteen year old adjusting to what was most likely his first extended experience away from home and mother rarely could see the humor of being rousted out of a warm bed by some thick-necked bully in a Smokey-the-Bear hat shouting, "Drop your cocks and grab your socks! Time to get up ladies!"

Even those who had been subjected to the harassment and hazing that often went hand-in-hand with membership on a high-school sports team weren't prepared for the streams of verbal abuse hurled their way.

"You needle-dicked bug fucker! What makes such a sorry-assed piece of whale shit like you, Private Numbnuts, think you have a right to be in MY army?"

But the shouting and threats were part of the training. The army's approach to taking young men and turning them from civilians into soldiers involved systematically taking away the individual's identity in order to make a team player, one who would not question authority but react instinctively to orders. A soldier who hesitates, who waits to consider his options, may soon find his moment of indecision has squandered those options. Be part of the group, react in a certain way, stimulus and predictable response, that's what the army wanted. Many of the young men who went through the experience saw the training for what it was and did not take the abuse to heart. Others, less mature, perhaps, or at least more vulnerable, did not take well to the training. So, after sixteen weeks of that sort of harassment, the individual who saw a career in that atmosphere could be rare indeed.

But Luster embraced this new environment. In a way, he felt he had to. The father he had never known, the man who had given his life for a higher cause in some foreign place in Europe in World War II, had gone through it and had become a soldier. A little verbal harassment and a little physical torment on the obstacle courses and forced marches was nothing Luster couldn't handle. It was the right thing, the honorable thing to do. And, besides, he wasn't going to be an infantryman. He had a technical bent, and his career was taking him into electronics as a radio mechanic. It was only a little bad luck, really, that had him assigned to an infantry battalion. He had been happy settling in to life with his unit in Germany when a levy came down with his orders for Vietnam. He wasn't too happy about leaving behind a new wife and an infant daughter, but it couldn't be helped. Not everybody in the army in Germany in 1967 got orders to go to Vietnam, but some did, and Luster was one of them. He could deal with it. Of course, he had expected assignment in the battalion's Headquarters and Headquarters Company (HHC); that's where the radio mechanics usually worked, there or in the battalion Tactical Operations Center (TOC) doing radio communications with the rifle companies, support elements, and higher headquarters. But when he got to the Manchus, Luster found there were no openings at HHC or in the TOC. All the radio operators there seemed to be guys who had earned their jobs the hard way, guys who had done their time in the field, perhaps gotten wounded, maybe even more than once, and with only a short time to go before their tours of duty ended, were assigned to these comparatively safe jobs as a reward for service rendered. It seemed fair enough to Luster, and he was sort of looking forward to life in the field. Though he wouldn't have said so, he wanted to see how he would react when he got shot at. He had to know, on a very personal level, if he could measure up and do what was expected of him just like his father had done. Being tested, he welcomed it as much as he dreaded it.

Henchman

Lieutenant Colonel John Henchman was given command of the Manchus on October 1, 1967. Just before shipping out for Vietnam, he had served in several staff positions at the Pentagon. Those jobs had given him a good background and valuable experience as an administrator. He was also a combat veteran, having served as a platoon leader and company commander with the Thirty-fifth Infantry Regiment in the Korean War. His service at Heartbreak Ridge, at the Punchbowl, and through the bitter winters on the Chorwon and Kumhwa Valley campaigns shaped his approach to leading men in combat.

Henchman saw his role as commander of a combat infantry battalion in very human terms, considering those in his command more like family, men he owed an allegiance to, rather than strictly as subordinates expected to follow orders and do what they were told.

He also had his own ideas about the right tactical approach to use in Vietnam. He believed fighting a guerrilla war meant different tactics than what official Pentagon doctrine described. He knew that trying to force-fit tactics designed to confront the Soviet Union in a conventional war of massed armies with thousands of tanks and infantry lined up on a thousand-mile front wouldn't work in the jungles and rice paddies of Vietnam.

His first few months with the Manchus proved his initial assessment had been right. He adapted to this new environment and rapidly developed his own way of doing things. One of his first observations about the way the battalion had been operating before his arrival was that the men were all carrying very heavy loads on their operations each day. The rucksacks they carried weighed fifty to sixty pounds, sometimes more. Henchman knew from his experience in Korea that there was no way an infantryman could fight weighed down with so much gear.

Henchman knew that to be effective, to accomplish the mission of finding and fighting the enemy, his Manchus must first and foremost be mobile, able to move quickly, and perhaps most important, they had to be flexible. They had to be ready to adapt to situations that changed rapidly. Sometimes that meant airborne assaults by helicopter; other times it meant going into an area on foot. The necessity to move quickly also meant that special thought should be given to the equipment each man would carry. The way to emphasize speed and agility was to minimize the load. Make sure each man had what he needed but no more. At times they would even leave their steel helmets behind and wear soft jungle hats instead. Henchman believed that the U.S. Army had plenty of helicopters for the heavy lifting when it came to ammunition, food, and other essentials. The thirty-nine-year-old lieutenant colonel called it the light fighter concept and dubbed his Manchus Henchman's Light Rangers.

Henchman's sometimes unorthodox methods at first met resistance from within the Twenty-fifth Division's chain of command, but higher headquarters soon were applauding the way the Manchus were operating and the success they were having in finding and engaging the elusive enemy. His style went down well with his superiors, so well that when the U.S. Army chief of staff, four-star General Harold K. Johnson, came to visit the Twenty-fifth Division on December 28, 1967, the division commander Maj. Gen. F. K. Mearns took him out to see the Manchus. General Mearns also spent New Year's Day with the battalion. The division commander clearly saw something he liked in the way Henchman operated. The Manchu commander's immediate superior, Colonel Fremont B. Hodson, commander of the First Brigade where the Manchus were normally assigned, shared that opinion. But the Hoc Mon area was the responsibility of the Twenty-fifth Division's Second Brigade, under the command of Colonel Raymond O. Miller a new arrival in Vietnam. The Manchus were to be placed under his operational control when they were sent to stop the rocket attacks around Saigon.

Colonel Miller was less enthusiastic about Henchman's style, which became apparent almost immediately, when the Manchu commander briefed him on how he planned to insert the battalion into the Hoc Mon district on February 25.

Henchman and his operations officer, Major Bill Roush, had planned a series of landing zones (LZs) for the troop-carrying helicopters to deploy the men. They would move in quickly, unannounced, and begin operations immediately, denying whatever enemy might be there any opportunity to prepare an unwanted welcome. When Henchman briefed him on the plan, Miller asked why there were no plans to prep the area with artillery strikes, the conventional tactics used by infantry forces in nearly all U.S. wars. Henchman explained that the Manchus had learned from experience that such preparatory fires served no real purpose because if the enemy wasn't there it was a waste of artillery shells, and if they were, then all the barrage would accomplish would be to let the enemy know where the troops were planning to arrive.

Colonel Miller did not like the explanation and

insisted that preparatory fires be used, and Henchman planned accordingly, while at the same time making a list of alternate landing zones should the prepped ones prove to be hot.

Even when there is the best coordination in such operations, there is always an interval between the time the last artillery shell explodes in a target area and the time the first helicopter can safely arrive. Any combat helicopter pilot will attest that it doesn't pay to rush it. And it had been the Manchu experience that, if enemy troops were close enough, there was the risk that the interval between the lifting of the artillery barrage and the arrival of the first troops would provide enough time for them to set up a hot reception for the Americans. So Henchman's plan to lay down a thick layer of smoke on the landing zone made sense. If any enemy troops had moved in to the prepped area, they were likely to open fire on the first helicopter they saw. And, as it happened, when that helicopter smoke ship made its first pass, it drew ground fire. Henchman immediately ordered the alternate LZ be used, and all four line companies were inserted without incident. The repercussions, however, would come later along with a chewing out for what Miller considered a violation of his orders and a missed opportunity to engage the enemy.

And so the operations around Hoc Mon began. None of the men in the battalion had any sense of when operations might end. Each day the operations went on, it seemed they might stretch longer and longer.

It was to be a hard and demoralizing time.

FOUR

The Enemy

You will kill ten of our men, and we will kill one of yours, and in the end it will be you who tire of it.

—Ho Chi Minh

Major Tu Nhut, the commander of the Quyet Thang Regiment with its three battalions of Go Mon guerillas, was aware of every Manchu movement right from the beginning. The intelligence unit of the regiment, the Cong-Cung - or Apple of a Parent's Eye, as they were nicknamed - was made up of a handful of men and women whose job it was to keep tabs on the enemy. In the Hoc Mon district they had an excellent network of informants already established. That's why the Cong-Cung intelligence officer, twenty-four-year-old Nguyen Van Phi, knew the Manchus' movements almost from the instant the first troop carrying Huey helicopters began arriving. Although many of the local residents had fled the area due to the heavy fighting that had taken place there since the Tet Offensive had begun a month earlier, there were enough stubborn, diehard farmers with loyalties to the Viet Cong to keep the intelligence flowing. The local population heard the artillery bombardment and then watched as the helicopter formations flew in the troops. In the days ahead, the civilian population would go about its daily activities, watching the Americans as they conducted sweep after sweep in the rice paddies, canals, and marshes of Hoc Mon district. What they learned they would pass on to Viet Cong intelligence gatherers like Nguyen Van Phi.

Phi moved freely along the fields and roads of the district, a pick axe over his shoulder and conical straw hat perched on his head. He had little trouble passing as a simple farmer moving to and from his fields. Even though he was of military age and should have been serving in the South Vietnamese military, he drew little suspicion. A birth defect that had left him with a cleft palate, and the facial disfigurement that went along with it, added to the persona he cultivated as a simpleton exempt from conscription by the Saigon government.

The Manchu intelligence resources, on the other hand, were woefully inadequate, which is not to say that the Americans had not tried. Since the mid-1960s the Pentagon had been aware that winning the war in Vietnam meant more than military success on the battlefield; they would have to win the support of the Vietnamese people, and if they could, then the intelligence they would gather about the communist insurgency would have real value. This battle for the "hearts and minds," as it became known, was embodied in a pacification policy to promote political, social, and economic improvements in the country. That meant the country's infrastructure would need strengthening. New schools, hospitals, agricultural programs, and the promotion of democratic processes would be essential. But these programs, when they were implemented, could not easily overcome the resentment the Buddhists of Hoc Mon felt for the Catholic leaders in Saigon, who, to them, seemed determined to impose Western religion on an Asian culture.

For the U.S. political leadership and the vast majority of American soldiers serving in Vietnam, the reason America was supporting the Saigon government was simple. They had come to the aid of an ally with whom they shared a strategic interest, that is, stopping the spread of communism. The American view was that North Vietnam under the leadership of Ho Chi Minh was intent on overthrowing the democratic government of South Vietnam in order to impose a communist dictatorship. If the North Vietnamese proved to be successful in Vietnam, then the rest of Southeast Asia would be vulnerable, too, and could end up falling to communism as well. The world was already divided into two camps: the free, democratic West led by the United States: and the communist dictatorships that had already swallowed up Russia and China. Communism could not be allowed to spread even further so that more of the world fell under its influence. Washington and most Americans believed the war in Vietnam to be at the very heart of America's interests. Better to fight communism in the jungles of Southeast Asia, the saying went, than on the streets of America. Few in Washington saw the war the way many in the Hoc Mon District did, not as a fight to impose a new political system on the people of Vietnam, but as opposition to a corrupt and unpopular regime that was not representative of them at all.

In the 1960s the population of South Vietnam was approximately 15 million, but only one-and-a-half million were Catholic. The vast majority, some 70 percent, were Buddhist. Despite their numbers Buddhists throughout the country had been relegated to the status of second-class citizens, a policy first promoted by the French when they were the country's colonial rulers. The Catholic Church was the country's largest landowner, and most of the Vietnamese administrators of the country were Catholic. It seemed clear that the South Vietnamese government would have to do something to bridge the divide between the rulers and the ruled, but there is little evidence to suggest they were so inclined. To the contrary, actions by the government in Saigon only contributed to the sour relations between the two. One of the worst events occurred on May 8, 1963, when a large crowd of Buddhists gathered in Hue to celebrate the 2527th anniversary of the birth of the Buddha. The South Vietnamese government saw the gathering as a threat, more of a political act of defiance than a demonstration of religious faith. The police moved in to try to disperse the crowds and eventually opened fire on them, killing one woman and eight children.

The Buddhists were furious and began a series of demonstrations against the government of Catholic President Ngo Dinh Diem. In an attempt to let the world know how strongly they felt about the South Vietnamese government, Buddhist leaders decided to ask for volunteers to commit suicide. What followed became one of the enduring images of the Vietnam conflict and one of the strongest symbols of Buddhist resentment of Catholic rule. A sixty-six-year-old Buddhist monk named Thich Quang Duc answered the call for volunteers. On a warm June day in 1963 he walked onto a busy Saigon street and sat down cross-legged in the middle of the road while a fellow monk doused him with gasoline. As film cameras rolled, Duc struck a match and set himself ablaze. It got everyone's attention.

If the Buddhists expected this dramatic gesture to soften the hearts of those in the government, they were wrong. Instead, Saigon responded to the suicide by arresting thousands of Buddhist monks. Many disappeared and were never seen again. By August of that year another five monks had committed suicide by setting fire to themselves as Duc had done. One member of the South Vietnamese government responded to these self-immolations by telling a newspaper reporter, "Let them burn and we shall clap our hands." Another offered to buy the gasoline for any Buddhist who wished to commit suicide.[10]

In such an atmosphere it was not surprising that the Buddhists of the Hoc Mon district were overwhelmingly opposed to the Catholics running the country and in many cases openly hostile to them. In Hoc Mon the Buddhist connection was especially strong with a Buddhist Pagoda that was both school and monastery for the boys of the district.[11] There were other reasons why the locals were often eager to join the armed resistance to the South Vietnamese government and their American allies. The Catholics had been given preferential treatment by the French during the colonial era and had become the rich and powerful of Vietnam. They were the landowners and businessmen. The Buddhists were the peasants.

But it wasn't just this conflict between the haves and have-nots of Vietnamese society that provided fertile ground for the Viet Cong recruiting effort. For there was also a huge core group who first organized to fight the Japanese in World War II, then successfully kicked out the French colonialists but remained unhappy with the outcome of the 1954 Geneva Conference that left the country divided. They had dreamed of a unified Vietnam and wanted it still. That guerrilla army, the Viet Minh, was, under the terms of the agreement

10. David Halberstam, New York Times (11 September 1963).
11. The Chua Thien Linh (Heavenly God) Buddhist Pagoda, built in 1958, was home to fifty-three monks.

on disengagement, dispersed. Some ninety thousand headed north, but several hundred thousand well-organized fighters and their sympathizers were still in place in the south. These men and women had thought the end of the war with the French would have brought a unified Vietnam under the leadership of Ho Chi Minh. So a whole new army wasn't raised; it simply changed names from Viet Minh to Viet Cong.[12] The term Viet Cong was used by the Americans to mean the irregular guerrillas they often encountered on the battle field. The name is a contraction of Viet Nam Cong San or "Vietnamese Communist," and it was given to the guerrillas by the Diem government. Those fighting that government called themselves the National Front for the Liberation of South Vietnam, or National Liberation Front (NLF) for short. The NLF was founded in 1960. By 1965 when American ground forces arrived these NLF fighters had seriously degraded the fighting ability of the Saigon government's army. This guerrilla army, of mainly illiterate or semiliterate men and women, had built a clandestine government and army with, quite literally, an underground network

---

12. "The ability of the Viet Cong continuously to rebuild their units and to make good their losses is one of the mysteries of this guerrilla war... . Not only do the Viet Cong units have the recuperative powers of the phoenix, but they have an amazing ability to maintain morale. Only in rare cases have we found evidences of bad morale among Viet Cong prisoners or recorded in captured Viet Cong documents." (Gen. Maxwell Taylor, briefing to senior Washington officials, November 1964).

of factories, hospitals, and supply systems that ran the length and breadth of the country. In five short years this hidden army had developed small-unit tactics that rewrote the textbook on guerrilla warfare. They were on the verge of defeating an army and bringing down a government that the United States had spent hundreds of millions of dollars supporting.[13]

By 1968 many of the residents of Hoc Mon felt far more allegiance to the insurgents of the Quyet Thang than they did to the South Vietnamese government. After all, their sons, daughters, fathers, and mothers were either active participants in the fight against the U.S.-supported government or had been. The local population was therefore happy to share information with Viet Cong intelligence gatherers like Nguyen Van Phi. Helping the South Vietnamese Army or their U.S. allies was out of the question. This disconnect between the South Vietnamese government and the local population meant that when North Vietnamese officers like Nguyen Ngoc Nham moved into the area to recruit fighters and organize a fighting unit, they found a receptive atmosphere.

With virtually no one on the ground to provide human intelligence about Viet Cong activity, the Americans had to rely on technology for the basics. They knew, for example, that the rockets being fired at Tan Son Nhut had to be coming from the Hoc

---

13. Frances Fitzgerald, Fire in the Lake (1972), p. 139. Little, Brown, and Company, Boston, Toronto

Mon District. Examination of the impact areas and calculations of the likely trajectory of the 122mm rockets the Viet Cong were using implied they had to be in that area. Radar from the airfield also picked up the rockets as they were fired, adding to the conclusion that the Hoc Mon area was the launching point. If there was other information available to the Americans, it was never passed on to the ground commanders who were given the job of finding and stopping the rocket attacks. As Henchman began preparing his plan for operations in the Hoc Mon area, he had been told that he might be facing a group already known to military intelligence as the Go Mon Battalion—perhaps 100 to 120 men. He had no idea that he would in fact meet a whole regiment, the Quyet Thang, with three Go Mon battalions of 120 men. Each Go Mon unit was set up in well-fortified underground positions all along a seven-kilometer stretch of the Saigon River. The Third Go Mon was positioned just north of the large bridge spanning the river at Phu Long. The First and Second Go Mon battalions were well concealed in the marshes and canals at the big bend in the river near the village of Ap Phu Dong, some five kilometers north of Saigon's metropolitan sprawl. Led by North Vietnamese Army officers, the Go Mon battalions of the Quyet Thang were a competent and effective fighting force, motivated by a deep hatred of the South Vietnamese government's ruling elite.

John Henchman had, of course, heard of the Go Mon, for the battalion had already met them on the battlefield several times, even before Henchman took command. Some of his officers and men knew them very well indeed, and they considered them to be a potent fighting force. Much of that respect came from the experiences they had had a little farther north and west along the Saigon River during an encounter at a place they will always remember as the Horseshoe.

FIVE

The Horseshoe

Are gods more ruthless than mortals?
Have they no mercy for youth?

—Charles Kingsley, *Andromeda*

In early August 1967 the Manchu battalion had only recently grown from three rifle companies to four with the addition of a new company, Company D. To avoid fielding a totally green unit made up entirely of new replacements with no combat experience, a decision was made to try another approach at building and fielding a new rifle company. The plan called for each of the existing companies to send one platoon of experienced men to the newly formed Delta Company, giving it a total of two rifle platoons of men with combat experience and one platoon of replacements with less than sixty days in country. Each of the existing companies would then bring themselves back up to strength with replacements. In theory, each of the four companies in the battalion would be 66 percent combat veterans and 33 percent replacements. The bulk of the new replacements arrived in Vietnam aboard the USNS *Barrett* during the first week in August and a few from the normal replacement channels, the Ninetieth Replacement Detachment in Long Binh.

The newly reconfigured battalion was fortunate in that it had no major engagements during its first few weeks of existence. All that changed on August 30, when they ran into, quite literally, the men of the Go Mon

The mission that day was a reconnaissance in force in the swampy area near the Saigon River not far from the main Twenty-fifth Division base camp at Cu Chi. The spot was in the enemy-dominated area known as the Iron Triangle. The Manchus had engaged an enemy force of undetermined size in that area on August 29. When reconnaissance spotted what was believed to be an entrenched Viet Cong battalion, senior commanders wanted to go after them. The enemy positions were found in an area where the Saigon River makes a big, almost circular loop near the place where it is joined by the Thi Tinh River some eight miles northwest of the village of Phu Cuong. Using tactics identical to those employed in the trench warfare on the Western Front during World War I, Division Commander Maj. Gen. F. K. Mearns planned a massive artillery bombardment and a series of air strikes on the suspected enemy locations. More than 2,000 artillery rounds and bombs were to be expended on this horseshoe-shaped area in the hours leading up to the arrival of the Manchus.

Mearns and his staff were confident that most of what they estimated to be a battalion of Viet Cong would be unable to withstand the heavy air and artillery strikes. So the plan that was developed called for the Manchu Battalion commander at that time, Lt. Col. Stanley Converse, to take his men into the horseshoe after the bombardment, do a damage assessment to judge how effective the massive shelling had been. The Americans would then take any survivors prisoner, and collect and destroy any enemy weapons found. Small pockets of resistance might be encountered, but the brass believed it would be nothing that would take more than a few hours to accomplish. As a result of this assessment, Converse planned accordingly, and ordered the Manchus to travel light. They carried no rations, no equipment to prepare shelters, and no extra ammunition.

At 0830 the first air strikes began pounding the heavily fortified positions of the Go Mon Battalion at their base camp in the horseshoe, followed at 0910 by a massive artillery barrage. Then the Manchus were sent in. As they approached the landing zone in the middle of the horseshoe, they got their first look at what they were heading into. What they saw was not encouraging. It looked like the surface of the moon. The bombardment had left hundreds of water-filled craters in the flooded rice paddies. But of more concern was that their wide-open landing zone was surrounded on three sides by heavily wooded areas with tree-lined embankments that could provide perfect concealment for an enemy.

At 0933 the first helicopters approached. At first there were no signs of the enemy, but as the LZ began to fill with helicopters and the first of the troops began offloading, the Go Mon fighters emerged from well-fortified underground positions and opened fire. Alpha Company, the first into the LZ, with half its force now landed, took cover behind the nearest rice paddy dikes and began returning fire. The Go Mon kept up their attack with disciplined, aimed, and accurate fire, pinning down the thirty to forty Americans now on the ground. For the Manchus there was no turning back. With men already on the ground, the only way to give them the support they needed was to get the rest of the battalion in there with them.

More helicopters began arriving with the remaining elements of Alpha Company and the Go Mon turned their attention to them. As long lines of green tracer rounds began pinging through the thin magnesium skins of their helicopters, the pilots began breaking formation. Some veered off to the left of the leading ships that were still hovering above the ground, dropping off their troops. Others came straight into the hot LZ following closely on the tails of the helicopters that had just unloaded. The result was that the remaining elements of Alpha Company were scattered throughout the area, unsure of exactly where they or the rest of the company was.

Incoming helicopters were still dropping off troops while those Manchus who could were periodically sticking their heads up from behind the dikes and firing across the empty paddy into a tree line some thirty yards away. The Go Mon never stopped firing back. They were showing no sign of having suffered much, if at all, from the intense bombardment. They had taken shelter in an extensive network of tunnels that, unknown to the Americans, ran for miles through the area. The tunnels, some more than thirty feet underground, had provided near-total protection, and the Go Mon Battalion was now emerging from the holes into heavily fortified bunkers and fighting positions that surrounded the LZ the Manchus had selected.

The initial Alpha Company elements now on the ground were not only taking fire from the tree line in front of them but from the left and right flanks as well. The combined roar of mortars, machine guns, and automatic rifles was deafening, and the Manchus began to take casualties as they lay in their exposed positions. The Go Mon showed their training and fire discipline, shooting only when they had a clear shot. It was a grim scenario. If anyone put his head above the dike, he risked being shot. And still the Manchus kept coming, offloading troops from Bravo Company into what had become a shooting gallery.

By 0948 all of Alpha and Bravo were on the ground. Miraculously no one had been killed, but two men from Alpha and one from Bravo were wounded. The situation was chaotic. The din was continuous; automatic- weapons fire from the Go Mon and the two

Manchu companies joined the roar of the mini-guns from helicopter gunships and the enormous explosions of 750-pound bombs and 20mm cannons from the F-4 Phantom jets that had also arrived on the scene. The airplanes were flying so close to the Manchus that red-hot 20mm shell casings were at times raining down on the men. The air support worked, however, at least well enough to allow Bravo Company to get off the LZ and onto higher ground where their movements were not so difficult and where they were less exposed.

At 1019 Delta was inserted in the same area where Bravo had landed. And again the Go Mon riddled their helicopters with automatic-weapons fire as the aircraft worked their way into the area. If anything, the ten helicopters bringing in the newly formed D Company drew even heavier fire than the two previous companies. The Manchus on the ground and in the sky watched as green and red tracer fire filled the air. Despite the noise of the helicopter's turbine engines and the clack of whirling blades, those troops still airborne could hear bullets hammering into the aircraft and in some cases tearing away great pieces of metal from the machines. The intensity of the fire meant the ten-ship formation again broke up, scattering widely across the landing zone as each pilot looked for a place to get down low enough for the troops to get out and then rapidly clear the area. All the while they were trying to avoid colliding with the other aircraft landing and taking off. The chaos of the scene was brought home graphically as one helicopter limped away from the hot LZ, the body of its door gunner dangling limply by the heavy canvas safety sling that attached him to the aircraft.

By the time the operation at the Horseshoe was four hours old, four Manchus were dead and twenty were wounded. The three companies were still pinned down, not far from where they had been when they had first arrived. The artillery and air strikes continued, seeming to hit closer each time. The Alpha Company commander, Capt. Thomas Lewman, ordered everyone up on their feet and over the dike they were taking shelter behind to charge the tree line across the open rice paddy. The company was pinned down, couldn't maneuver, and was taking casualties. The only option was to get out of the open rice paddies that three-quarters of the battalion had flown into. So the men of Alpha Company did as they were asked. They rose to their feet and advanced on the tree line upright and exposed, assaulting on line in a scene reminiscent of more ancient wars. Somehow it worked. The Go Mon abandoned their bunkers and moved deeper into the trees to pre-planned fall-back positions. But the relief was brief. For no sooner had Alpha reached the tree line than the Go Mon began returning a heavy volume of fire from deeper in the trees. More attacks by gunships were called in to keep pressure on the Go Mon and so it continued.

Night was coming, and with it rain and a chilling fog. Then, as suddenly as it had started, it stopped. After more than eight hours of continuous shooting the battle was over. The Go Mon had simply broken contact and melted away into the tunnels and underground bunkers of the Horseshoe, taking their dead and wounded with them. It had been a brutal confrontation for the Manchus. Nine men were dead (one would die two days later), and thirty-six were wounded.[14] The 187th and 188th Assault Helicopter Companies suffered one dead and nine wounded. Of the twenty-four helicopters that flew repeatedly into the landing zone, twenty-two of them took multiple hits. The troop carriers had been shot up so badly that there were none available to bring in Charlie Company as planned to confront the Go Mon guerillas. They would get their chance six months later.

14. Vaughan Shaw Morgan, Charles R. Wilkerson (Alpha); Tom J. Bagenstose, Douglas Coats, Benjamin D. Coy, Terrence Joseph Kudro, Roy H. Leach, Robert W. Morgan, John Joseph Pinder (Delta). Dennis Erwin Gabbert (Alpha) died September 1, 1967 from wounds received in the Horseshoe battle.

SIX

Hoc Mon

Rejoice, O young man, in thy youth.

—Ecclesiastes 11:9

Charlie Company was the first Manchu company into the LZ in the Hoc Mon area on February 25 and took the lead as the battalion began to move north up highway 248. They moved several miles before splitting off to the left and then off to the left again on a little trail that cut through a heavily wooded area. The men also saw the place was laced with irrigation canals. Third platoon leader, 2d Lt. James O'Laughlin, had given his men a briefing of what to expect and had warned them that the area they were going into was dangerous and that they could expect contact. So far, however, there had been no sign of the enemy, and the men were starting to relax.

Pfc. Wayne Holloway, the new guy who had only been with Charlie Company for a little over a month, started to feel a little more comfortable once they were off the helicopters and moving. They were deployed in a defendable tactical formation with every reason to believe they would be ready for what might come. Holloway was getting a bit more confident that, at least for this day, there wasn't going to be any action. But after they had been moving along that little road there for a short time, they began taking fire from their left flank. Everyone got down. Automatic-weapons fire coming from the woods just off the road. Lieutenant O'Laughlin shouted, "Assault left." The men responded immediately. Holloway couldn't help thinking, "It's just like they taught us in training." Everyone got on their feet, turned and faced to the left, and began an immediate advance, firing rapid single fire into the jungle. As they weaved around the trees, the separation between men began to disappear here or widen there. At one point Holloway and Pfc. Larry Walden ended up so close together that as Walden stepped ahead of him and began climbing the bank of a canal, Walden's M-16 began spitting hot brass down Holloway's neck.

The whole company was putting out a heavy volume of fire, but neither Holloway nor Walden knew how effective it was until a small palm tree off to their right suddenly crumpled and fell. Whoever they were facing in that tree line was most definitely still shooting back. Still the men continued forward until ordered to halt after they had gone some fifty yards into the tree line. They immediately took cover on the ground and waited, not really knowing much about what was going on. Then the order came to withdraw, and the men headed back to the road. It was there Holloway saw his first casualties. One Manchu had apparently gotten ahead of the line of advance and had been shot in the arm by one of his own men. Two medics attended to the wounded man, then disappeared into the woods. They reappeared a few minutes later carrying someone else on a stretcher. Holloway saw right away that it was Dennis Gulich and that he was dead from a gunshot wound to the head. The twenty-year-old from Detroit had had just twenty-two days left before he was due to go home.

To Holloway and the others it didn't seem fair. He had gone through so much and was so close to having it all behind him. What was he doing out in the field still, being such a short timer and a weapons-platoon man to boot? Guys in weapons weren't supposed to be out on sweeps with the regular rifle platoons; they were supposed to be in some base camp or defensive position with their mortars. But on this operation things were different. The mortar men had been told that army intelligence was using radar to pinpoint where the Viet Cong rockets were coming from. If the Manchus were firing their mortars at the same time, it would confuse the radar operators. For the Hoc Mon operation the mortars were left behind, and the mortar men became riflemen.

In addition to having lost a friend, the weapons platoon had also lost a leader, and leaders were in short supply. Holloway's own squad leader, Sgt. John Withers, had recently finished his one-year tour and had already rotated back to the States. It was

depressing. There were frayed nerves. The remaining
NCOs seemed sometimes irritable. Everyone was
complaining about the discomfort of life in the field.
They were traveling light, unbelievably light in the
opinion of Holloway and the other weapons-platoon
members. The only personal items they carried were
a razor and a blanket or poncho liner. Everything else
was left back at the base camp.

The operations the next day, February 26, were much
the same. The Manchus moved out from the temporary
night-time defensive perimeter they had set up and
began a sweep, looking for the elusive Second Go
Mon Battalion and the stockpile of rockets they were
using in attacks on Tan Son Nhut. None of the men
knew exactly what to expect. Would they find anyone?
And if they did, would it be just a couple of guerrillas
sniping at them from a distance or would they come
across the main force—the whole damn battalion of
Viet Cong? There was simply not enough intelligence
regarding Viet Cong activity in the area for anyone to
know whether the Go Mon battalion would confront
them in large numbers, harass them with sniper fire,
vanish into the maze of tree-lined canals and marshes
that dotted the Hoc Mon area, or ambush them.

Each American soldier learns something about
planning and executing ambushes during basic
infantry training. They know what is required to plan
and execute an ambush on an enemy force. They have
been taught that successfully springing an ambush
will almost certainly require keeping your own forces

hidden to maintain the element of surprise, and maybe even letting the first enemy soldiers walk completely through the killing zone of your ambush in order to allow the main body into it. The Manchus also knew that to get caught in the killing zone was extremely dangerous and that it was imperative to not walk into such a trap. The best preventative was to send out elements in front of and to the sides of the main body as it moved through enemy territory. Such security was critical. These men would likely spot an ambush before it could be sprung on the main group. It was standard operating procedure to send out a point man or two and a flank man on either side before any group set out from a defended position. Every Manchu knew it, and they did it every time they moved anywhere.

These security elements had the key job of finding any enemy ambushes before they could be sprung. It was a dangerous job, and companies would take turns leading the battalion, so that the risk was shared evenly. Within the companies, the three rifle platoons would also routinely alternate leading the company. The platoons themselves would also rotate each of the three rifle squads, in a further effort to spread out the risk. But these were not hard and fast rules. Some men wanted to walk point, preferring to trust their own skills and instincts rather someone else's. Others would say they just liked it better than being back with the main group. Several of the platoon leaders in Charlie Company routinely walked point, wanting to see, first-hand, what was going on.

Every infantryman was alone, in the sense that in open terrain like that around Hoc Mon they kept at least ten yards between men, sometimes more, the reasoning being that by dispersing that way they prevented the enemy an opportunity to simply open up on a group with a burst of automatic-weapons fire, killing or wounding the whole group of men. Each man would have to be targeted individually. Even with that sort of spacing, though, there was a sense of being part of the larger group and a feeling that should they be surprised by the enemy and come under fire, well, what would be the chance that they themselves would be the first target? Chances were that someone else would be shot at first, and the rest of the group would have a chance to take cover.

The man walking point cannot afford to think that way. He is not part of the larger group. At times being as much as twenty-five, even forty yards ahead of the main body, he is on his own. With a skill that comes only from experience, he must watch each step for booby traps: a bamboo twig lying out of place on top of a rice paddy dike where no bamboo is growing, a glint of dew on a monofilament line stretched across the grass. At the same time he is scanning the trees and bushes around him for any movement, and not just at ground level but up in the treetops as well. He must sense what is normal and what is not without even knowing exactly what is out of place. At times it is a smell that is cause for concern, the faint hint of a wood fire or scent of rice cooking when there is no village nearby. Sometimes it is a sound. The shuffle of boots and clanking of equipment that inevitably accompanies the movement of eighty or one hundred men in the company following him is background noise for the point man. The sounds of his own breathing and swish of his fatigue trousers moving through grass are unwelcome clutter in his ears. He listens for the chirping of birds, the lowing of water buffalo, the chatter of children's voices and the clatter of everyday life in the villages he passes. He also listens for an unnatural stillness when those sounds stop. He listens to himself. He listens to an inner sense that tells him of danger. And he must keep that focus, that concentration with every step he takes. Everyone else depends on him.

These basic tactics of small-unit operations were well understood by the Viet Cong, too. Just like the Americans, the Viet Cong would sometimes send small groups of men, two or three, away from their major encampments, men who would be used to provide early warning of approaching Americans. These outposts would have the job of engaging the Americans to slow them down so that the larger Viet Cong body could escape. In that scenario, the American point man would be the target. They knew that by shooting him, they could slow the Americans, who would come to the aid of their downed comrade. It would mean the main group of Americans would avoid being ambushed but at the cost of the point man and, quite likely, anyone who tried to come to his aid. That is what happened on February 27. On that day, Charlie Company was the lead company for the Manchus and Second Platoon was out front.

The Manchus had set out in a column of two files, with a man well out in front of the main body providing point security and one man off to each side of the formation near the front to protect the flank. If the Go Mon battalion had set up an ambush, the point man or a flanker would find it, allowing the Manchus the opportunity to wheel around to the enemy's flank and attack before the rest of the company got into the killing zone.

Charlie Company was heading into open country, eager to get away from highway 248 and its bridges, obvious choke points where they would be forced together, forming what for the Go Mon battalion would be an appealing target. But a wide-open rice paddy had plenty of risk associated with it, too. About the only precaution to be taken was to spread out, increase the space between individuals, let the point man get well ahead of the main group, and hope he would see some sign if trouble lay ahead.

The Go Mon snipers waited until Second Platoon was well out in the middle of a wide-open rice paddy but before the two point men, Sp4c. Ken Aleshire in the right file and Sp4c. Denny Dubendorf in the left, had almost gotten to the hedgerow marking the canal where the Viet Cong troops lay waiting in small bunkers. The snipers opened up with a burst of automatic-weapons fire. Aleshire and Dubendorf went down right in the middle of the wide-open rice paddy. The rest of the men in Second Platoon began returning fire toward the hedgerow to allow the two point men a chance to get out of the paddy and behind the protection of a dike. Dubendorf scrambled out of the paddy, but Aleshire didn't move.

For the rest of the platoon, it was impossible to tell what they were facing. Perhaps this was one of those times when the Viet Cong had just opened fire with the intent of only maintaining contact for a few minutes, just enough to slow down the Americans and let the attackers escape. Or maybe they were still there, waiting to shoot any rescuers coming forward to help the wounded man. It was impossible to know which situation Second Platoon was facing. Someone had to get to Aleshire, see if he was still alive, and then get him back to a safe area where he could be given first aid and evacuated. First Lieutenant Louis McFarland and Sp4c. Mitchell Sek decided to try to get to Aleshire and pull him back, but this turned out not to be a hit-and-run attack. The sharpshooters were still there waiting, and both McFarland and Sek went down in a burst of automatic-weapons fire the moment they left the protection of the dike.

After several hours, artillery strikes on the tree line had their desired effect. The Manchus of Second Platoon moved forward and found the enemy positions now abandoned. They recovered the body of Ken Aleshire and set about evacuating Louis McFarland

and Mitchell Sek, both of whom were wounded but still conscious. Lieutenant McFarland was even giving instructions to the men treating him, telling them who to attend to first and how to go about getting organized to bring the med-evac helicopters in. Mitchell Sek sat up briefly as he waited for the arrival of the helicopter that would take them to the Twelfth Evac Hospital in Cu Chi. But both men had lost too much blood and fell into shock. Two more Manchus were lost to the Go Mon Battalions of the Quyet Thang.

During that fight, Battalion Executive Officer Major Bill Roush was on the ground traveling with Bravo Company and witnessing a similar scenario play out. They were walking along a rice-paddy dike just off highway 248 when someone opened fire on the head of the column. The point man, Pfc. Robert McCollum went down. Again, no one could tell if he was alive or dead, but everyone knew someone had to go get him and pull him out of his exposed position: he was lying right in front of the hedgerow where the shooting was coming from. Roush, Sgt. Dave Ruggles, and Sp4c. Dennis Wagner went forward while the rest of the company stayed strung out along highway 248. The men on the road, with a clear view of the efforts being undertaken to get to McCollum, put down suppressing fire as Wagner managed to crawl up to the hedgerow some distance away from the Go Mon shooter. He took cover behind a tree and then, hoping he had picked the right moment to leave the cover of the dike, went up and over it and slid into one of the many drainage

ditches in the area. Wagner followed the ditch up to
the point near where McCollum was lying. Trusting to
luck once more, Wagner reached up to grab McCollum
and pull him over the dike and down into the canal
with him, but the Go Mon shooters were watching and
waiting. A burst from an AK47 hit Wagner in both
arms. He fell back into the ditch. McCollum still lay
exposed in the open.

Sgt. Dave Ruggles and Major Roush made the next
attempt. Roush had plenty of experience with just that
sort of thing. On January 18, he had managed to pull
off a similar rescue when another man had gone down
in an exposed position. He had pulled it off another
time, too, on January 5. Just knowing that Roush
was with them made the men of Bravo Company feel
better. If anyone could get McCollum, Roush could.

Perhaps the Go Mon sniper had moved to a new
location while Roush and Ruggles moved into position
and now had a better angle to shoot at the men. Or
maybe Ruggles and Roush were just too exposed.
Neither made it. Just like Wagner, Ruggles was hit and
badly wounded in the arm as he reached for McCollum.
Bill Roush, one week short of the end of his third tour
of duty in Vietnam, was shot and killed as he peeked
over the last rice paddy dike that lay between him and
the lifeless form of Bob McCollum.

The difficult terrain and accurate sniper fire received
every day while in the Hoc Mon area was very hard on
the battalion. One could not imagine operations here
being more deadly than in War Zone C, but they were.

The loss of Bill Roush on February 27 had everyone in the battalion "down", including John Henchman who had not only lost his gifted operations officer, but a close personal friend. For Henchman, the loss of any Manchu was keenly felt, but the loss of Roush was especially difficult. Henchman was desperately tired from months of endless combat in War Zone C, and saddened by the heavy loss of life his battalion had sustained there before being ordered to the Hoc Mon area with little time to prepare his soldiers for a new mission.

To top it all, he was continually frustrated with his inability to work in harmony with the Second Brigade commander. Henchman repeatedly asked for the same kinds of support he had enjoyed in War Zone C when attached either to First or Third Brigades—a command and control helicopter when needed and priority of artillery fire when he was in contact. The Second Brigade denied him this support in most cases, giving priorities to the three battalions which were assigned to the Second Brigade.

The day after Roush was killed, Bravo Company had been engaged along one of the Canals leading to the Saigon River when, with darkness falling and the tide rising, Henchman had ordered Bravo and Charlie, which had been deployed in support of Bravo, to pull a few hundred meters back from the area to a higher, more defensible terrain which was a couple feet above the tide line. Henchman knew that within a couple hours the area Bravo and Charlie Companies were in would be submerged under several feet of water. It would be no place to spend the night, especially surrounded by an enemy with intimate knowledge of the area. Colonel Miller was furious, demanding to know why Henchman had broken contact. "You been out here Colonel? I did not break contact!—the VC did. The water in that area will be three to four feet deep in another hour. I will not order these dog tired soldiers to stand all night in water up to their asses. That would be an insane order for me to issue."

With the deaths of Roush, McCollum, McFarland, Aleshire, and Sek, the losses for the battalion had grown to ten dead and dozens wounded in just three days in Hoc Mon. In the 151 days Henchman had been in command in the tough jungle areas of War Zone C and in Hoc Mon, in daily contact with a determined and wily enemy, the Manchus had suffered 138 dead and 731 wounded.[15] Henchman had come to hate Vietnam.

---

15. Ibid.

Lt. Col. John Henchman,
commander, 4th Battalion 9th
Infantry, 25th Infantry Division
October 1, 1967-March 2, 1968.
Photo courtesy of John Henchman.

Maj. William Roush
Manchu operations officer, killed
in the Hoc Mon operations while
trying to rescue Pfc. Robert
McCollum on February 27th,
1968. He was awarded the
Distinguished Service Cross for his
role in the Hoc Mon operations.
It was the second time he was
awarded the medal for actions
while serving with the Manchus.
Photo courtesy of John Henchman.

Nguyen Van Phi
photo from 1968 while serving as
intelligence officer for the Quyet
Thang.
Photo courtesy of Nguyen Van Phi.

Bravo Company crossing one of the
many bridges spanning the dozens
of canals in the Hoc Mon District.
Photo courtesy of Todd Dexter.

Manchus moving out down highway 248 in
preparation for a search and destroy mission in
the days prior to the March 2nd ambush. Many
civilians remained in the Hoc Mon area despite the
fighting, complicating operations.
Photo courtesy of Todd Dexter.

SEVEN

March 2nd

A professional soldier understands that war means killing people, war means maiming people, war means families left without fathers and mothers. All you have to do is hold your first dying soldier in your arms, and have that terribly futile feeling that his life is flowing out and you can't do anything about it. Then you understand the horror of war. Any soldier worth his salt should be antiwar. And still there are things worth fighting for.

—General H. Norman Schwarzkopf

The times the battalion was operating out of a semi permanent location such as a fire-support base (FSB), so-named because of the artillery batteries that would be located there, were the best the Manchus could hope for, short of assignment to the division base camp in Cu Chi. What amenities that existed for a regular infantry battalion were available at the FSBs. Daily resupply would bring all the critical items like ammunition and the food in the form of C-rations, Korean War–vintage packaged and preserved food. But because FSBs were less transient in nature, there would also be luxuries such as tankers filled with fresh, good tasting water, hot meals in the evening and sometimes in the morning, mail, and sundry packs. Sundry packs were wonderful. They were big plastic bags full of candy bars, shaving kits, tooth brushes, cigarettes, insect repellent. And they were all free. Few knew or cared where they came from. Most Manchus thought they couldn't be supplied by the U.S. Army, because the stuff in them was so good and useful.

At an FSB the troops could build more substantial defenses than they could anywhere but the major base camps that were home to thousands of support personnel. Solid sandbag bunkers six or eight feet long and sometimes even tall enough to stand up in could be built. These could have roofs made of perforated steel planking topped with several layers of sandbags to create solid defensive positions. Small sleeping areas could be set up next to and sometimes in the bunkers themselves. They usually were nothing much more elaborate than a lean-to type shelter built from plastic ponchos, but they kept the men out of the rain. An air mattress added a degree of comfort not possible when sleeping on the ground.

But the Manchus were not operating out of a fire support base in Hoc Mon. Here facilities were simple night defensive positions that offered little protection from enemy attack or from the elements. Frequent floods added to the already high water table and meant that any hole dug in the ground would soon fill with water. The men had a choice: dig a hole big enough for your body to fit into, watch it fill up, and spend the night up to your neck in water, or forget about a hole and just lie on the ground. Doing the latter would mean your fighting position would be far more exposed and you would still be wet when the tide began moving up the Saigon River, through the canals, and filling the rice paddies to within a couple of inches of the tops of the dikes. The earthen walls of the dike, usually several feet thick and a couple of feet high, were good protection from small-arms fire. The rice paddies themselves were usually rectangular in shape, 75 to 100 yards long and the same distance wide, bounded on all four sides by the earthen dikes. A company could set up a defensive position that would span several rice paddies, with positions spread out along the dikes and four-man listening posts set up several hundred yards beyond this perimeter to provide early warning should the enemy try to attack. But sleeping in the water-filled paddies was misery itself.

And so were the Manchus deployed in Hoc Mon. Each company set up its own night defensive position, assigning one of the three rifle platoons to ambush patrol responsibility each night. The whole battalion was spread out across about a square kilometer of countryside on both sides of highway 248.

They were getting hot meals in the evening resupply but breakfast was c-rations, bad tasting water purified with Halazone tablets and not much more. Adding to this more Spartan atmosphere was the very nature of the operation itself. All four line companies, Alpha, Bravo, Charlie and Delta, were conducting daily sweeps and night ambushes. Normally a company would set up in a night defensive position, then send two of its three platoons out on a sweep. The platoon left behind would rest up for night ambush. The duty rotated between companies, so that every fourth day was night ambush. The sleep deprivation from having been up all night was made bearable by the "day off" given to the platoon the day after their turn on ambush. That was how it usually went but the Hoc Mon operation was different.

All four companies were involved in the sweeps every day, and since they were not set up in any particular place there were no "days off." Each company would establish a night defensive perimeter, send one of its rifle platoons out for night ambush, tear down the perimeter at first light, and all of the platoons would then set out for the day's sweep. No downtime at all. It was fatiguing. A platoon coming back from night ambush patrol would only have time for a quick C-ration meal while the platoon leader got a briefing from the company commander on the operation for the day ahead.

Such was the normal routine for a regular infantry battalion like the Manchus. They had no mechanized vehicles, no tanks or armored personnel carriers. They were not like the elite paratroopers, who had the pride and esprit de corps characteristic of airborne units. They weren't highly trained experts in jungle warfare. Although they were a disciplined group that had trained together in Alaska and Hawaii when the battalion first arrived in country in 1966, they, like almost every other infantry battalion were different now. Before the end of the first year of their deployment in Vietnam, the Manchus had become like most infantry battalions—a collection of replacements. Most of the riflemen were draftees who had undergone eight weeks of basic training and eight weeks of advanced infantry training; then it was off to Vietnam. Few had any experience in garrison duty where they would have had the opportunity to get to know their officers, NCOs and the other members of their squads. Most had only a few months in the army before they found themselves with a line rifle company in the field. This reality held true for everyone in the battalion, not just for the newly arrived privates. The NCOs were not much different. Although some were career soldiers with a half dozen years of military experience behind them, many others had been promoted through the ranks during their months in Vietnam, a practice that was both a plus and a minus with regard to morale. The men were glad to see competence rewarded but did not relish the notion that the promotions usually came when the new sergeant had only a few months left in country. As much as they were personally happy when one of their sergeants had finished his tour and was on his way home, they missed his leadership. The NCO leadership positions were like musical chairs; few squad leaders or platoon sergeants served longer than six months in their positions. All of this was part of the Department of Defense policy that each U.S. Army soldier ordered to Vietnam would receive a one-year assignment. As the enlistments of the original members of the battalion ended, they would leave Vietnam, and their positions would be filled by individual replacements.

Most of the officers assigned as platoon leaders had little experience in leadership positions and rarely any combat time before coming to their assignments. By 1968 some of the captains and senior first lieutenants assigned as company commanders and platoon leaders may have been back for their second tour of duty in Vietnam, but for most it was their first and only leadership position in combat.

By the middle of 1967 the entire Manchu roster had turned over, and the battalion was seeing a steady stream of men coming in as individual replacements for those whose tours had ended. Each change meant a different mix of individuals in a company, platoon, squad, and fire team. While that should not have posed significant problems, the constant state of flux in the makeup of the units meant that even the best groups were constantly working to build the cohesiveness a unit needs.

Then there was the manpower problem that the replacement policy created. The date for the end of the year-long tour of duty was unique to each individual, and while this should not have posed a problem—that is, each departing individual would have his own replacement—in practice things worked out differently. Often an individual would finish his tour and leave days, even weeks, before a replacement arrived. An infantry company, which on paper should have had more than 120 men in it, more often was comprised of ninety men, or fewer as it awaited replacements or return to duty of the wounded and sick.

By the time March 2, 1968 rolled around, Charlie Company fielded eighty-two men of its own, with ten attached - artillery observers and an engineer squad from Alpha Company Sixty-fifth Engineers who would be called on to blow up rockets or other enemy weapons. They were an average infantry company, but they were about to experience something extraordinary.

The relationship between Manchu Battalion commander John Henchman and his boss, Second Brigade Commander Raymond Miller, had not improved. On the evening of March 1, Miller had taken the unusual step of flying out to Hoc Mon in person for a meeting with Henchman on the plan for the next day. Henchman outlined an operation that would have the battalion moving from highway 248, which ran through the middle of their operations area, east toward the Saigon River. They would be going into an area that division intelligence said showed numerous signs of Viet Cong activity.

Miller said no. He issued Henchman new orders telling him to move south along the axis of the road, as far as the ARVN compound, two kilometers to the south, to carry out a search and destroy mission west of the road, being careful not to destroy any civilian structure, and seize objectives in order to regain the contact which Miller believed the battalion had broken off the day before.

Henchman had already briefed the company commanders on his original plan so, with the last of the light fading from the sky, he called them together again and formulated a new plan. He told them that rather than sweep east toward the river, the battalion would concentrate on the west side of the road where Bravo Company had fought the day before in a firefight that had cost the lives of Pfc. Budrow Bass of Jonesville, Louisiana, and Pfc. Bennie Ksiazek of Gary, Indiana, and had left four other Manchus wounded.

Miller had made it clear that he thought if the enemy was to be found, it would be to the west of the road, concealed somewhere in the marshes and tidal canals that criss-crossed the area. So the Manchus would try to re-initiate contact with what intelligence believed was approximately one battalion of either Viet Cong or North Vietnamese Army that was somewhere in the area.

The plan Henchman then developed, and Miller

approved, called for Alpha and Bravo companies to
secure a bridge designated number 11, which was located
on the outskirts of the village of Ap Nam Thanh, and
a location near where Alpha and Bravo had established
a night defensive position on the evening of March 1.
Charlie and Delta companies would then move south,
passing through Alpha and Bravo to the next bridge,
spanning canal 12. Alpha Company would then fall in
behind Delta to join the other two companies as they
moved south down the road. Once abreast of their
objectives to the west, all three companies would turn
to their right flank. Then, spread out along highway
248 some 700 yards or so, they would march off the
road and into the rice paddies and begin a sweep due
west to an area where they thought they might find the
enemy. The turn to the right would result in a battalion
formation in which Charlie Company would be
furthest south on the left end of the formation, Delta
would be in the middle, and Alpha on the right. Bravo
Company was to be held in reserve.

Three air strikes on likely enemy positions had
been planned to begin at 0730 and end at 0900,
when artillery barrages would begin hitting all three
objectives that Alpha, Charlie, and Delta Companies
were to sweep.

The three rifle companies were to be in position
and ready to begin their sweep at 1000. The relatively
late hour was chosen to coincide with low water, since
a number of canals had to be crossed. The companies
would move in column as they marched down the

road, then, once in position, would turn right 90 degrees, spread out to keep a good interval between men, and sweep the rice paddies and hedgerows in one long line. And, as was the battalion SOP, specific security measures would be taken once they began moving through unsecured areas. As the companies moved in these areas they would move on both sides of the road in the first line of trees or along the first line of cover that would provide cover and concealment or, if cover wasn't available, at least concealment to the unit, providing it with flank security.

Later on the evening of March 1, Henchman modified the orders, requiring that Charlie and Delta Companies be in their attack positions at 0900, not 1000, in order to be ready should the tide be low enough to begin the operation. Tides have played an important role in military operations in Vietnam for more than a thousand years. As far back as 938 A.D. the storied Vietnamese general Ngo Quyen had successfully fought off repeated invasions of the armies of China's Quing dynasty, using the tides to his advantage, luring his enemy into areas that would dry out in the ebbing tide and leave the powerful ships stranded or holed from spikes not visible at high water. Similar Chinese invasions in 981 and 1288 were also repelled by taking advantage of this natural phenomenon. Any foreign army intent on operating in Vietnam needed to take the tides into account. They would play a role in the events that unfolded on March 2 as well.

U.S. intelligence believed that the enemy forces in

the area were the group they knew as the Go Mon battalion. As the Manchus had learned during their earlier encounter at the Horseshoe, they knew the Go Mon to be well-trained, disciplined, and aggressive. What the intelligence reports did not contain was detailed information about the size of the force or where they were deployed.

In fact the Viet Cong did not have a battalion (120 men) hidden in the swampy land adjoining the Saigon River. They had a regiment, some 360 men under the command of Major Tu Nhut. Major Tu Nhut had taken command of the regiment, the Quyet Thang, when it was formed. It was composed of veteran troops of the First and Second Go Mon Battalions as well as survivors from other units that had suffered heavy casualties in the initial fighting in the Tet Offensive. This latter group formed the new Third Battalion.

The Quyet Thang Regiment was led by officers of the North Vietnamese Army. The line soldiers were local volunteers. By early 1968 the men of the companies of the First and Second Battalions knew each other well, many of them having served at least three years together. First Lieutenant Nguyen Ngoc Nham commanded First Company of the Second Battalion. His career had begun in 1950, when as a sixteen-year-old he took up arms with the Viet Minh to fight the French. After the French defeat at Dien Bien Phu on April 25, 1954, he had wanted to return to his family home in Ben Tre province in the Mekong Delta. But he was called to Hanoi instead and spent the next ten years training and studying in North Vietnam's military schools. On July 10, 1964 he was ordered south, where he would receive orders on his role in the fight against the Americans.

Lieutenant Nham spent fifty-seven days making his way down the infamous Ho Chi Minh trail with the members of the 316th Division of the People's Liberation Armed Forces. On arrival he set about organizing the Second Battalion Go Mon. Other North Vietnamese officers were given the task of forming the First Battalion Go Mon. Their name, Go Mon, came from the area on the outskirts of Saigon where the Viet Cong soldiers were to be recruited. Go, from the town of Go Vap on the near northern outskirts of Saigon, and Mon, from the town that was the nearby district headquarters, Hoc Mon.

From a guerrilla force of approximately 5,000 at the start of 1959, the Viet Cong ranks grew to about 100,000 by the end of 1964. The number of infiltrators alone during that period was estimated at 41,000. The growth of the insurgency reflected not only North Vietnam's skill in infiltrating men and weapons, but South Vietnam's inability to control its porous borders, Diem's failure to develop a credible pacification program to reduce Viet Cong influence in the countryside, and the South Vietnamese Army's difficulties in reducing long-standing Viet Cong bases and secret zones. Such areas not only facilitated infiltration, but were staging areas for operations; they contained training camps, hospitals, depots, workshops, and command centers.

Many bases were in remote areas seldom visited by the army, such as the U Minh Forest or the Plain of Reeds. But others existed in the heart of populated areas, in the "liberated zones." There Viet Cong forces, dispersed among hamlets and villages, drew support from the local economy. From such centers the Viet Cong expanded their influence into adjacent areas that were nominally under Saigon's control.[16]

Lieutenant Nham had no trouble finding volunteers, all of whom were united in their desire to get the Americans out of their country. The way Nham saw it, he was fighting for his country, to protect its sovereignty and independence, just as he had done in the fight against the French. He saw the Americans as just another, newer version of the French who had colonized and occupied his country for more than 150 years. To him, the issue wasn't a fight for a political system. He knew little and cared little about politics. He wanted the foreigners gone.

The Go Mon battalions lived and fought in and around the region that gave them their name. Most often they, and the local villagers who knew them, called them the Otters, because they seemed to live more in canals and water-filled bunkers than on dry land. They were well supported by the local population, which was overwhelmingly Buddhist and had an active hatred of the Catholic-dominated Saigon government.

16. "The U.S. Army in Vietnam," American Military History (1988), p. 619. Government Printing Office, Washington.

The Go Mon had scored major victories during its history but had also suffered major losses as well. In preparation for the Tet Offensive of 1968, they were to play a major role in the offensive against Saigon and were given the job of attacking the Headquarters of the general staff of the South Vietnamese Army (ARVN). Despite arriving late at their assigned objective in the opening hours of the offensive, the Second Go Mon managed to enter Gate 4 of ARVN headquarters at 0700 and take control of parts of the compound including the Foreign Language School. They held their ground until February 1, when under the pressure of repeated attacks by helicopter gunships and coordinated assaults by both an ARVN parachute regiment and marines, they were forced to withdraw.[17]

The casualties suffered by the Go Mon that first day were rapidly replaced by new recruits, including several teenage girls and one fourteen-year-old boy.

On the morning of March 2, Henchman again briefed his company commanders on the operation, including the time change. He also arranged for a helicopter reconnaissance flight for all three company commanders who were to be involved in the sweep. They would over fly the area in the early morning hours so each could become as familiar as possible with their objectives and the terrain they would be required to move through.

17. Ho Khang, The Tet Mau Than 1968 Event (2002), p. 70. The Gioi Publishers, Hanoi

Ordinarily, an infantry battalion commander would have also had a command-and-control helicopter available to him for such an operation. But on March 2 no such support was planned, due to a critical shortage of such C&C ships in the second brigade. That meant that once the helicopter used for the reconnaissance flights left the area before the operation began, Henchman would travel on foot, near the head of his battalion, between Charlie and Delta companies.

But as Charlie Company passed his location as it began moving into position, Henchman was in conversation with the brigade artillery liaison officer. He decided to leave with Delta Company instead and eventually catch up with Charlie before they got to their attack position. Everything was set.

The First and Second Go Mon Battalions of the Quyet Thang Regiment had other plans for the Manchus.

EIGHT

The Ambush

*If you have tears, prepare to shed them
now.*

—William Shakespeare, *Julius Caesar* (III.2)

Dawn on Saturday, March 2, 1968 brought clear skies
and the promise of another sunny day. To Pfc. Wayne
Holloway it seemed like the weather was going to
be a little bit nicer than they'd been having recently.
It wasn't as humid as it had been, and it felt like it
might be a little cooler, too. Things always seemed
better in the light of day, and there was some civilian
traffic on the two-lane road that paralleled their night
defensive perimeter, enough to give the appearance
of normalcy. Farmers appeared to be heading out
to work the rice paddies and fruit orchards that had
been tended by local Vietnamese for as long as anyone
could remember. Jackfruit trees, star fruit, papaya, and
bananas grew together in shady mixed orchards that
lined the east side of highway 248. To the west of the

road were rice paddies and marsh. This area of wide-open fields surrounded by hedgerows was known as the Red Beetle Military Zone to both the American military planners and the Go Mon Battalions of the Quyet Thang Regiment. Over the years the guerilla fighters had carved out a sophisticated network of tunnels running from hedgerow to hedgerow that linked together underground bunkers, medical clinics, and sleeping areas.

The Manchus were to move out early so as to be in position at 0900 for their sweep into the Red Beetle Zone, but final preparations still needed to be made for the day's operation. To make sure there was no confusion about the new plan that the Brigade Commander had ordered, Henchman arranged for an aerial reconnaissance of each objective for each of the company commanders. An OH-23 observation helicopter was at the battalion command post by 0800. The two-seater began flying the company commanders out one at a time to have a look at the terrain.

As they conducted their reconnaissance Henchman reflected on all that had happened. He was still depressed over the loss of his friend and right-hand man, Bill Roush. His black mood had not been improved by having had yet another run-in with his brigade commander the night before. As they conducted their reconnaissance, Henchman was discussing his frustrations with Bill Roush's replacement, Major Raymond Massey, who had arrived just two days before. Together with the Battalion

Intelligence Officer, they were working on maps in the front yard of the abandoned Vietnamese house in which Henchman and a couple of his staff had spent the night. During the night, Miller's operations officer had ordered Henchman out of the house because Miller's Liaison Officer had reported it was a Buddhist "shrine." Henchman believed it wasn't and that it was a typical Vietnamese house with a small area reserved for Buddhist worship. It rankled Henchman that in the face of major tactical and support difficulties and issues, Miller and his staff would focus on such trivia.

At the other end of the chain of command, Wayne Holloway and fellow weapons platoon member, Alvin Cayson, stood along the side of the road, waiting for the word to move out. They munched on some of the fruit they had picked from one of the many small trees in the orchards that lined the east side of the road. The round, smooth skin of the pommelos they had taken, with their thick husk and the sweet, grape-fruity meat, were a welcome treat after the uninspiring C-rations that the men of Charlie Company had had for breakfast.

C-rations were never good even when warmed over a piece of burning C-4 a dangerous plastic explosive. And that was something else—burning C-4. Holloway was starting to get used to handling the dangerous plastic explosive, although he was still a little leery of the practice. He had been told by the older guys in weapons platoon that it was alright to burn the stuff but that it was very important to remember that once lit it should be allowed to burn itself out. Trying to stomp out burning C-4 could have explosive, even lethal results. Holloway didn't know of anyone who had blown himself up that way, but it was part of the lore that somebody knew somebody whose friend knew someone that it had happened to. It seemed to make sense that such a thing could happen—it was explosive stuff.

Most of the veterans in Charlie Company were accustomed to being around dangerous material, the newer guys less so. Holloway and some of the others were making the transition from the training environment, in which all firearms, ammunition, and explosives were carefully controlled, to the one out in the field, in which cautions seemed more lax. Back at Ft. Polk, Louisiana, where many of them had gone through Advanced Infantry Training, none of the dangerous weapons were accessible without the explicit permission and direct supervision of a senior NCO or officer. Out in the field in Vietnam, they slept with the stuff. In addition to the personal weapons they carried, either an M-16 automatic rifle, M-60 machine gun, M-79 grenade launcher, 45-caliber pistol, or 12-gauge shotgun, each man also carried four hand grenades, often a claymore mine, and sometimes a light anti tank weapons (LAW), the disposable anti-tank weapon the Manchus most often used against enemy bunkers. Each man knew it to be a deadly load but had to put aside thoughts of how fatal a moment's carelessness could be.

Such concerns were not foremost in their minds on the morning of March 2, however. It had been another uncomfortable night. In addition to the misery mosquitoes always brought with them, the Hoc Mon area added a new level of irritation, as the rising tide had begun to flood them as they lay on the ground, wrapped in their nylon poncho liners. And then there were the casualties: twelve dead in the battalion in the past six days.[18] It seemed like every time they went out something bad happened. It was wearing on everyone's nerves.

Wayne Holloway shared that same uneasiness as he prepared for the day's sweep. He had been told that the battalion was going back into the area where Bravo Company had been hit the day before. Bravo had lost two men. The rumor in Charlie Company was that Bravo had also lost a machine gun in the incident and that battalion commander John Henchman was not happy about it. Losing any weapon was bad news, but losing one as powerful as the M-60 was even worse. It didn't pay to dwell on what the Viet Cong could do if they got their hands on it.

---

18. February 25 - B Co. - Sp4c. Daniel Callahan, North Reading, PA, Sp4c. Verlin Holderly, McCurtain, OK – C Co. Sgt. Dennis Gulich, Detroit, MI, February 26 – D Co. Sp4c. Phillip Lucas, Los Angeles, CA, Pfc. Anthony La Rocco, New York, NY – February 27 – B Co. Pfc. Robert McCollum, Marietta, GA – C Co. Sp4c. Kenneth Aleshire, Philadelphia, PA, 1st Lt. Louis McFarland, Santa Barbara, CA, Sp4c. Mitchell Sek, Chicago, IL, HHC Maj. William Roush, Houston, TX – B Co. Pfc. Budrow Bass, Jonesville, LA, Pfc. Bennie Ksiazek, Gary, IN.

Sfc. Frank Hettiger's normal job was as platoon sergeant for Charlie Company's third platoon, but due to the recent casualties and chronic shortage of senior NCOs, he was serving as field first sergeant for the whole company. The initial movement out of their night defensive position called for the company to deploy in a column with a file on either side of the road. Third platoon, commanded by 2d.Lt. James O'Laughlin, would lead. Behind them would be the company's headquarters element with company commander Captain Willie Gore, radio telephone operators (RTOs) Danny Young and Danny Luster, engineer Aristides Sosa, and the artillery forward observer along with Senior Medic Ron Slane. First Platoon, commanded now by SSgt. Arthur Minjarez following the death of Louis McFarland, was next in the order of march. First Lieutenant Frank Tinkle's second platoon was the trailing element.

Hettiger positioned himself between First and Second Platoons to keep the senior leaders of the company dispersed throughout the column, not bunched up.

It was getting close to 0900, and Charlie Company was late. Captain Gore had not returned from the aerial reconnaissance flight that each of the rifle-company commanders had taken. Delta Company had already moved out. Charlie would have to catch up. When Gore was finally back on the ground, he wasted no time ordering Charlie Company to saddle up, and they did, not exactly running but not moving exactly cautiously either, trying to catch up with Delta Company. Delta had gotten to the approach to the bridge spanning canal 11, then stopped to wait for Charlie Company. It was at that point that Charlie caught up and began moving through Delta, the point crossing the bridge and scurrying forward at a good pace in the hope that the company could make it to their line of departure on time. Once they got to the line of departure, they would swing to the right and advance, on line, through the open fields and dry rice paddies toward their objective.

As he walked along the highway, Sergeant Hettiger began to wonder about security. On several occasions in the past few days, the battalion had out-posted the road; out-posting is a simple, if time-consuming way of securing an area. A company in column with a file on either side of the road would begin moving forward but after the first man had traveled a short distance, perhaps only fifteen or twenty meters into the unsecured area, he would peel off the road, move ten to fifteen meters to the side, and take up a defensive position. The next man would continue forward on the road another fifteen or twenty meters before peeling off toward the flank to do the same thing. The leapfrogging would continue until the whole company was off the roadway, providing security for whoever was to follow them. The unit following could then move through the area in security, a cordon having been established along both flanks of the roadway. It was an effective but time consuming way to move.

As Hettiger walked along highway 248, he began to worry and wonder why no one had been sent out to secure the flanks on both sides of the road. Sending out one man as flank security was not a foolproof way to ensure the safety of the unit, but that individual, if sufficiently far enough toward the head of the file, might discover someone lying in ambush before the whole company walked into the trap. Perhaps they were in an area that had been secured the night before, and maybe the plan was for flankers to be sent out once Charlie Company had gotten further down the road, nearer the planned line of departure for the day's operation. It was not normal procedure to omit flank security. Perhaps there was some reason for doing so this morning.

As Hettiger was considering those concerns, he noticed that the civilians who had been mixed in with the American formation as it moved south down the road had suddenly stopped and begun heading back the way they had come. That was odd. Had they seen something? Did they know something was up?

Charlie Company kept going, crossing the bridge that spanned canal number 11 and on another 300 meters or so, then up and over the bridge at canal 12. Still Captain Gore put no flank security out as his men kept up the pace moving rapidly down the road to make their line of departure position on time. His company was now more than 500 meters beyond the area the battalion had secured the previous night. It seemed Gore did not see, nor did he sense, that his men were walking into a trap, one that had little to do with the flank security Hettiger worried about and everything to do with surprise and overwhelming numbers. The commander of the Quyet Thang Regiment, Major Tu Nhut, had no clear idea what the Manchu plan for the day was. Two of the three battalions in his regiment had not encountered them in the six days the Americans had been in the area. Only his third battalion, based near the Phu Long bridge, had engaged the Manchus as they operated in an around the Red Beetle Military Zone. But Nhut knew where the Americans were and that as long as they stayed in the area, he would be unable to carry out what was his main near-term objective: to attack and destroy the nearby ARVN garrison. It was his fear that the Americans were trying to reinforce the ARVN, and that would complicate matters. It is always difficult to attack a well-defended position. The last thing Nhut wanted was for it to be reinforced by a battalion of American infantrymen and the powerful arsenal of artillery, helicopter gunships, and fighter bombers they could call on for support. He worried the Americans were coming to support the ARVN. He could not afford to let that happen.

Nhut formulated a plan to stop them and in the early morning hours of March 2 called together the commanders of the First and Second Go Mon Battalion to give them their orders. They were to move out immediately and engage the Americans as they began moving south toward what he thought was the Manchu objective, the ARVN garrison. At 0400, two Go Mon battalions began moving north from their positions in the swampy area near Go Vap on the outskirts of Saigon to their ambush site just south of bridge 12.

Although Nhut's Quyet Thang Regiment had seen much action during the initial phases of the Tet Offensive a month earlier and had suffered substantial losses, they were still an imposing force. Most men carried the Kalashnikov AK47 assault rifle. A few were armed with the older semi-automatic SKS rifle. Perhaps a dozen men in each battalion were armed with either RPG-2 or RPG-7 rocket-propelled grenade launchers, and many of the men also carried the grenades for the weapons. They also had half-a-dozen medium machine guns.

The force of more than 200 Viet Cong soldiers of the First and Second Go Mon Battalions arrived at their objective while it was still dark and immediately began taking up their positions. Concealment was their main goal, and noise discipline was imperative. Knowing they were within just a few hundred yards of the Americans in their night defensive positions, the Viet Cong soldiers could not afford the risk of being detected by the commotion caused by extensive digging and fortifying of positions. They took cover where they could find it. A few men set up in an abandoned grass and mat hootch on the west side of the road; others set up in groups of three or four behind gravestones in several small family plots. Some dug shallow firing positions in the soggy soil of the rice paddies but most simply gathered palm leaves or dead vegetation and covered themselves with it. Almost all of them were in makeshift positions within ten or fifteen yards of the road.

The plan was simple: First Battalion deployed on the east side of the road, Second Battalion on the west. They staggered their positions across from each other to lessen the risk of hitting their own forces when they opened fire. They spread out from the canal bank on the south end of bridge 12, where they set up several positions east and west of the road in order to cut off the head of the American formation and stop any reinforcements from getting to the ambush killing zone once the ambush had been sprung. The two Go Mon battalions were spread out some 400 yards to the south where a bend in the road gave a clear view of the roadway all the way to the bridge. There they set up a machine gun. The gunner was told to wait until the first American was right in front of him before he opened fire. That first machine gun burst would be the signal for the Second Battalion men on the west side of the road to throw off the palm leaves that were concealing them and open fire. One minute later, First Battalion was to join the shooting. After fifteen minutes the main forces were to withdraw from their positions, First Battalion to take cover in the swampy area along the banks of the Saigon River to the east, Second Battalion to move to hedgerows several hundred yards to the west. Only the men in the positions along the canal at bridge 12 were to remain in place as a blocking force in order to keep American reinforcements from attacking as their main elements withdrew. It was a simple plan, using surprise and numerical superiority. It required little in the way of coordination, and once set in motion would operate without additional instructions.

NINE

The Killing Zone

The thundering line of battle stands,
And in the air Death moans and
sings…
—Julian Grenfell, "Into Battle"

Pfc. Darrell Wheeler was the first to die. The point man was killed instantly in the initial burst of machine-gun fire, which also claimed the life of the man behind him, Pfc. Clifford Stockton.

Pfc. Augustine Lugo, the third man in the right file of third platoon, managed to swing his M-79 grenade launcher in the direction of the tree line to his right, where he thought the firing was coming from, and got off one single, 40mm, high-explosive grenade in the direction of the trees before a second burst of machine-gun fire began chewing up the asphalt and dirt and pieces of Lugo before dumping him unconscious on the edge of the road.

Squad leader and machine gunner, Sp4c. Thomas

Mork, and his ammo bearer, Pfc. Andy Rodgers, were right behind Lugo. They hit the ground, and Mork immediately began returning fire with the M-60. Mork's heavy volume of fire seemed to be keeping the Viet Cong's heads down, but even so Rodgers couldn't seem to move without drawing fire. At the rate he was firing, Mork would soon run out of ammunition if Rodgers couldn't get more belts to him. A couple of dozen yards behind Rodgers and Mork, Pfc. James Elliott was also down on the road, looking for but not finding any cover.

Then, while the men still had no real sense of what was happening and exactly where the enemy machine gun was located, automatic rifles opened up from a second position at the right front. Then fire began from behind them, too, from positions even closer, maybe a dozen yards back in the small trees that hugged the edge of the left side of the road. There was no going forward, no going back. The enemy was on both sides of the road, and they had set up interlocking fields of fire that covered the entire 400-yard long stretch of road between the men at the head of Charlie Company and the bridge they had just crossed. All but a handful of the company was trapped inside the killing zone.

Charlie Company commander Capt. Willie Gore raced for cover in the orchard to his left but found none. Gore and his command group had been walking down the center of the road when the ambush was sprung. While they stood completely exposed like the rest of the men, they were not initially targeted, as the machine guns and automatic rifles were raking the files that lined both ssides of the road. Everyone dove to the ground for cover. Gore, one of his RTOs, Danny Young, and the members of his command group nearest him went down on the east side of the road, Sp4c. Danny Luster on the west. Gore told Young to call Third Platoon sergeant Jesse Lunsford to see if he could find out what was happening. Maybe Lunsford had an idea where the fire was coming from.

Gore used his second radio to get Henchman to tell him that Charlie Company was under intense RPG fire from both sides of the road.

Danny Luster was alone on the opposite side of the road from Gore and like everyone else he was laying flat on his belly. The deafening noise made it impossible for anyone to hear spoken commands, but Luster didn't wait for an order. His radio was tuned to the artillery net, and he immediately tried to call in artillery support. He rolled onto his left side, brought the radio handset to his right ear, keyed the push-to-talk switch, and screamed "Manchu fire mission! From my position XT843…"

That was as far as he got. The copper jacketed-bullet of an AK47 slammed into his right bicep, knocking the handset from his hand. A second bullet hit his head just above his right ear. The impact knocked his helmet off and left him momentarily dazed. Ignoring the pain in his right upper arm and head, he rolled to his right side and reached across his body with his left hand for the handset that lay just beyond his now useless right hand. A third bullet struck his left arm just below the elbow and scraped along the bones of his lower arm before exiting just above his watch band, tearing out a handful of soft tissue as it went and again knocking the handset out of his hand.

Then, *wham, wham, wham, wham, wham!* Five hammer blows in his back and side. His PRC-25 radio deflected the first three bullets, but two slipped below the radio's metal housing and dug deep into his left side just above the liver.

The radio, now useless, was only causing problems. Luster knew it was the radio the enemy was after and that if he was to have any chance, he would have to get away from it. He wriggled out of the radio pack, bounded to his feet, and raced toward his company commander on the east side of the road. He only got a few steps before a sixth bullet hit his right ankle, sweeping his legs out from under him and sending him sprawling on his back on the asphalt just feet short of the slight depression Gore and the rest of his command group were in.

If Luster had harbored any hopes that he might survive despite the six bullet wounds he had already suffered, they were erased when the RPG struck. The three-and-a-half pound projectile struck his midsection just above his right hip. It glanced off his hip bone, raked his lower abdomen, and tore open a gash, four-inches wide and nearly a foot long. It took skin, some of the muscle of his abdominal wall, and a large section of intestines as it went, the hot gasses of the rocket propellant cauterizing the flesh and soft tissue with a sizzling sound. The grenade did not explode, but the force of the blow lifted Luster off the ground and flipped him over face-down on the road. A seventh bullet struck Luster's left side at an angle, collapsing his left lung and fracturing the vertebrae in the middle of his spine before exiting above his right hip. Again the impact of the bullet was enough to roll him over. He was again flat on his back, staring up into an almost cloudless sky and bleeding from eight serious wounds. He was still conscious.

Third Platoon RTO Rudolph Love could hear one of Gore's RTOs, Danny Young, calling him on the radio, but when he answered there was no response. He tried again to establish contact but could not. Then things were too busy to worry about the radio. Love was fortunate to have been near a banana tree when the shooting started. He dove to the ground and found himself in a shallow depression behind the tree. Pfc. William Pockhus lay nearby, bleeding from a gunshot wound. Love rolled over next to Pockhus, pulled his sterile dressing from the pouch on his web gear, and wrapped it as tightly as he could to try to stop the bleeding.

Love thought the firing had to be coming from the tree line somewhere off the right side of the road and began looking for something to shoot at. He had eighteen rounds in the magazine of his M-16 and one in the chamber. He fired eight times into the trees before he, too, was hit.

Everywhere the men of Charlie Company had been diving toward what seemed the only protection there was, the shallow depressions that lined both sides of the road. No sooner had they hit the ground than the whole road erupted as Go Mon soldiers fired volley after volley of RPGs down the length of the asphalt.

A hundred yards behind where the body of point man Darrell Wheeler lay, his platoon leader 2d. Lt. James O'Laughlin, was frantically urging his men to get up and move, to assault the distant tree line where the worst fire seemed to be coming from. But assault right made no sense to O'Laughlin's men. Assault right meant standing up into a totally exposed position and then, somehow, advancing across yards and yards of open rice paddy with no cover of any kind. It seemed it could not be done.

Pfc. Dan McKinney thought the lieutenant was crazy. Even though the roar of the firing and the explosions made his commands impossible to hear, his gestures made it clear he wanted everyone to get up. All Dan could think to do was get the lieutenant to give up the idea and to get himself back down on the road for his own safety. Surely he could see it was nuts to try to move across that open rice paddy. So McKinney got up and ran to O'Laughlin, trying to get him to understand that what he was asking was impossible and that he had to get back down on the road. O'Laughlin ignored him, continuing to shout for the men to get up. McKinney gave up. He turned back toward the place he'd come from on the other side of the road, threw himself back down to the asphalt and, he hoped, out of the line of fire. He needed help. The next time he looked O'Laughlin was down on the road, too. McKinney could tell from the awkward way he was sprawled across the asphalt that he was dead.

Now that the lieutenant was gone, there was no one trying to get the platoon to act together. Every man still alive was on his own. What McKinney couldn't know was that similar dramas to the one that had just played out with Lieutenant O'Laughlin was being repeated along the length of the road as man after man was shot. In the space of only minutes the ambush had destroyed Charlie Company's ability to work as a unit. Now it was every man for himself.

With his platoon leader dead and no sign of anyone else to turn to, McKinney felt helpless, unsure of what to do next. He briefly considered heading for the trees that bordered the left side of the road. But getting up to run even the ten or twelve yards might be fatal. Then, as he lay on his belly, half on and half off the asphalt surface of highway 248, the Go Mon ambushers found him. *Slap, Slap*, the soles of his feet feeling the burning fire of the shrapnel as it tore into him. *Slap, Slap*, first his right leg, then his left jerked hard to the side from the force of the third and fourth pieces of jagged metal tearing into the flesh of his calves. The next chunk of steel cracked against his skull, knocking off his helmet and creasing his scalp along his right temple. The seventh blow, this time from a bullet, hit him square in the back, collapsing his lung. Dazed and in pain he struggled to pull off his equipment, hoping that he could use his rucksack and canteens to build some sort of barrier between himself and the bullets. He was still conscious but only just. He was aware that someone was next to him, telling him to try to stay calm and that he would be okay.

As he tried to assess how badly McKinney was hurt, Medic Ron Slane could not have been sure he himself believed the assurances he was giving. McKinney was bleeding everywhere, and his sucking chest wound needed immediate attention. His breathing had become rapid and shallow and his pulse weak as his remaining lung tried to do the work of two. The veins on his neck were standing out, the trachea pushed to one side. The standard battlefield treatment for the wound would have been to take plastic-covered dressings and cover the holes in his chest, front and back. But even that simple procedure was not possible because the bullets were still flying, and getting himself into a position where he would have the leverage to turn McKinney's body over would expose Slane even more than he already was. Slane would have to work lying next to McKinney. From the large pools of blood that had started to form on the asphalt it was clear there were other wounds that would need attention. But most of the blood was reddish-black, not the dangerous bright red color characteristic of arterial bleeding. Slane would just have to take his time and go over the wounds one by one. First, though, he would need to try to calm McKinney down. He pulled a vial of morphine from his aid bag and prepared to inject it in the muscle of McKinney's thigh. It wasn't the best option; it would have been far better to get the drug into a vein with some sort of drip where he could monitor McKinney's condition and control how much of the drug he was administering. That would have been fine in some field hospital, but Slane was dealing with another reality and the options were extremely limited. It is never easy for any medic to have to make such decisions, but Slane, like the others, knew that it was all up to him, that there was no one to consult with or to ask advice. He was the one who had to make the call. It was up to him to figure out what to do so he decided on a course of action. He would calm McKinney down, ease his pain, and slow his breathing. If he didn't do so immediately, the medic knew he would lose his patient to shock. Without further delay, he jabbed the needle through the cloth of McKinney's pant leg and into the flesh of his hamstring, thumbing the plunger down and sending the pain killer into the muscle. In short order the wounded man's rapid panting began to slow, and, perhaps, his risk of lapsing into shock had been reduced. Maybe it was already too late for McKinney, but at least the morphine would make his last moments painless.

A short distance away, nearer the rear of the column, Pfc. Alvin Cayson lay unhurt, propped up on both elbows and firing furiously, peppering the distant tree line with 40mm high explosive rounds from his M-79 grenade launcher. Though only a single shot weapon that had to be broken open and reloaded after each projectile was fired, the M-79 could be used to deadly effect in the right hands. To his right and behind him some ten yards, Pfc. Wayne Holloway was giving as much support to Cayson as he could, his M-16 snapping off rounds in short, three- or four-round bursts. Holloway could see Cayson's grenades exploding as they hit the canopies of the trees in a tree line some 100 meters to the west, showering everything within a five meter radius with shrapnel. The Manchus had come to expect that in such situations there might be snipers up in the trees. They'd had experience with snipers doing just that before. They had seen them tie themselves in the canopies though they could never quite understand what sort of motivation it took for a man to take a rope and tie himself up in a tree. Maybe it made some sort of sense—get wounded, you won't fall—but the ones the Manchus had come across were all dead, their bodies dangling from those ropes. It just looked strange. Holloway hoped Cayson's grenades were finding their mark.

The deafening noise of more than 200 rifles and machine guns of the two Go Mon battalions, firing all at once, coupled with the explosions of RPGs, hand grenades, and the M-79 rounds Cayson was laying into the tree line made it impossible for the two men to communicate other than by gestures. Neither wasted much time trying to coordinate their actions, but both knew instinctively their only chance was to eliminate the nearest Viet Cong who were targeting them, and there seemed to be so many of them. Where had they all come from? It seemed their only defense was the sheer volume of fire they were pouring into that tree line.

Holloway carried sixteen magazines of M-16 ammunition, each loaded with eighteen rounds. Cayson carried a large canvas bag filled with more than two dozen high explosive "eggs." Both men kept at it, knowing that their firing was the only thing keeping the automatic weapons and machine guns from finding them. They also knew that they needed help before they ran out of ammunition. When that happened they would be lying there defenseless with no cover, no protection. The Viet Cong would be free to pick them off one by one.

First Lieutenant Frank Tinkle heard the machinegun off to the right at the head of the column. At first, the young lieutenant thought that it was something the lead element would take care of. His second platoon had only just started crossing the bridge on highway 248 when the shooting began, and it was perhaps 400 yards away from the action. Perhaps he would get a call on the radio from his company commander with an order to start moving to the right to try to flank whoever was firing the machinegun at the lead elements of Charlie Company. He never got a chance to find out what the commander might have wanted to order, as seconds after the firing began the trees on the left side of the road erupted. One of the first bursts of automatic-weapons fire raked the surface of the bridge, hitting Tinkle in both legs and knocking him and the man nearest him, medic Pfc. Jose Alvarez, to the ground. Then it seemed like almost simultaneously the shallow depressions on each side of the road exploded. Command-detonated mines, RPGs—something had exploded in the faces of anyone seeking shelter there.

Sp4c. Denny Dubendorf was right behind Tinkle and Alvarez. He knew the surface of the bridge offered no shelter. In fact, it seemed that the bridge was acting like a funnel and that all the bullets were coming down the road straight at him. Somehow the initial barrage left him without a scratch, but he knew he had to move. He could see both Alvarez and Tinkle had already been hit, and it looked to him that they were beyond help. He jumped over their bodies and ran forward. His first and only thought was to get down off the bridge and seek shelter under it.

His path took him forward and to the left and, without realizing it, directly toward three Viet Cong riflemen from the first platoon of First Lieutenant Nguyen Ngoc Nham's First Company, Second Go Mon Battalion, which had been positioned in the thick grass along the bank of the canal at the foot of the bridge. The sight of the American running straight at them must have startled the Viet Cong, for there was a moment's hesitation. Then they opened up on the darting figure. Dubendorf just ran, in a curving

arc off the road, down the sloping earth foundation
of the bridge, and straight past the Viet Cong. As he
ran, he could hear AK47 rounds hitting the bridge
support and feel ricocheting pieces of concrete zinging
past his ears.

Somehow he made it down the bank. He dove
into the canal and turned around to face back in the
direction he had come. The three Viet Cong who had
been shooting at him were out of their positions and
were coming toward him, and it seemed like they were
not more than ten yards away. Dubendorf froze where
he was, laying half in and half out of the canal, his
body submerged, only his head and shoulders resting
in the grass and mud of the bank. Turning to run across
the canal and possible shelter would turn his back to
his attackers and didn't seem a good option. Getting up
was equally risky; as he could see no place that it made
sense to go. Then the world went white. Something just
feet from his face exploded, lifting him off the ground
and throwing him back into the water. When he came
to his senses he realized that against all logic he was still
unhurt. A mine, grenade, RPG, something, had gone
off in his face, and still he was unhurt. Dubendorf also
knew he could not stay in that canal with three Viet
Cong just feet away.

As he considered his options, he was shocked to
find he was not alone. Pfc. Leroy Williams was right
there with him in the canal. Williams had been behind
Dubendorf on the bridge and had jumped from it
directly into the water. Williams looked up and saw

a narrow space between the bridge supports and its earthen foundations. He scrambled up into the small slit as Dubendorf stood waist deep in the canal, ready to provide cover. The three Viet Cong who had followed him were, for some reason, not shooting. But before Dubendorf could clamber out of the water to join Williams, the three enemy soldiers appeared again. As Dubendorf watched, he saw an arm rise up, then arc through the air. *Ploop*, a hand grenade splashed into the canal next to him and exploded. Still, amazingly, the shrapnel had missed. His ears ringing from the two explosions in the space of a few seconds, Dubendorf scrambled up out of the canal to join Williams in a small cubby-hole formed between the I-beams of the bridge and its foundation. As he sat in the hollow of one I-beam, his legs braced on the other, he took stock. One canteen on his pistol belt had been emptied by a bullet that went through it. There were two bullet holes in his pant leg, but he was unhurt.

From where Rudolph Love lay, he could see that somehow First Platoon machine gunner Sp4c. Nick Cutinha and his ammo bearer, Pfc. James Mathis, had managed to move up from their original position some 100 yards back and were continuing to work their way forward through 3rd platoon toward the head of the column. How the machine gunner had the nerve to stand up in the face of all the fire was almost impossible to understand, but the effective fire Cutinha was putting on the Viet Cong machine guns that had been methodically hitting every man in the area seemed more like a miracle. Porky's presence was making an impact. And it just felt good for the wounded to know they weren't alone, that there was someone there doing something. Bullets were still flying everywhere, but they did not seem to be the result of aimed fire, or at least not from the nearest enemy. Cutinha and Mathis kept trying to make their way forward to the head of the company. They managed to crawl up to a small hootch. The hootch wasn't any real protection, but it did provide some concealment. The noise from Cutinha's machine gun added to the wall of sound engulfing the men, but it did feel good to see someone able to do something instead of just lie there and bleed. For someone lying on the road wounded and defenseless, the throaty roar of Cutinha's M-60 was beautiful.

The next time Love looked up he could see that Cutinha had left the protection of the hooch and had begun making his way forward, trying to get even closer to where it seemed the worst of the enemy machine-gun fire was coming from at the head of the column. It wasn't possible to know for sure, since Cutinha was on the opposite side of the road. Perhaps he was trying to get to a position where he had a better angle. But this time Mathis, the ammo bearer, stayed behind. To Love it looked like Mathis froze. Love called for Mathis to come join him in the ditch but the twenty-six-year-old New Yorker didn't leave the flimsy cover of the straw hooch. Love, feeling the pain from the gunshot wounds he had already suffered, stayed where he was.

Further back down the road from Love, between Third Platoon and First, Captain Gore was still working to get a sense of what was going on. He couldn't talk to anyone in the lead platoon. He knew he had to get help to them, to relieve the pressure somehow. SSgt. Arthur Minjarez was in command of First Platoon, second in the order of march, and the most senior man near Gore, just a few yards behind him. Gore called out to him and began signaling Minjarez to swing his men around to the left and break out of the killing zone of the ambush. He thought that maybe Minjarez would be able to flank the enemy that was pouring so much fire onto the third platoon at the front of the column.

Minjarez took up a position on the side of the road. No sooner had he begun putting out fire toward the right flank than his M-16 jammed. As he frantically worked to clear the stoppage, he saw two Viet Cong running through the cane field on the left side of the road. He succeeded in clearing his weapons, chambered a round, and turning toward the running figures began shooting. It was at that point that Gore radioed and told him to try to move to the right side of the road, where it now seemed the fire was most intense. Minjarez passed the word to move out and began crawling across the road himself. When he reached the other side, he looked back. It seemed his men were unable to move, as the firing had picked up from the left side of the road. He yelled for his men to find cover, crawled down a slight embankment to a muddy ditch, and kept on firing himself. For the next several minutes Minjarez traded fire with a Viet Cong position just twenty-five yards away, until his rifle became completely jammed and full of mud. All he had left to fight with were the four hand grenades he wore strapped to his web gear. He used them all, lobbing in the direction of the Viet Cong position, but as far as he could tell, it had no effect and the AK47 fire continued, punctuated now and then by the powerful concussions of hand grenades the Viet Cong were throwing at him.

From where he lay just off the left side of the road Gore could see Minjarez, no more than ten yards away, trying to get his people to move. But before anything happened, another wave of explosions tore through the whole company. It was either a simultaneous detonation of more claymore mines or a coordinated firing of rocket-propelled grenades. It was impossible to tell. The explosions and the machinegun fire, which had never let up, continued with such an intensity that those not already dead or wounded were pinned down and unable to move. The firing and explosions were so disorienting, everyone on the road was still having difficulty trying to find out where the shooting was coming from.

John Henchman had been standing at his command post talking with the brigade's artillery liaison officer Lt. Col. A. M. Dean when the first shots were fired. This meeting had been scheduled the night before between Henchman and Miller's Direct Support

Artillery Battalion Commander, Dean to settle the issues the Manchus had been having in getting priority of fires since arriving in Hoc Mon when the battalion was in close contract.

Henchman had only moments to take in the fact that someone had opened up with automatic weapons when the intensity of the firing rose to levels he had never heard before. Even at a distance of more than 200 hundred yards, the sounds of the battle were deafening, the biggest, loudest fight Henchman had ever experienced. He ran to the road to see if he could make out what was happening. From where he stood, most of Charlie Company was not in sight, only the trailing element that had not yet crossed bridge 12 was near enough, and he could see some of them. There were ten or twelve men lying on the road near the bridge. He could not tell if they were dead or alive.

In the meantime, Delta Company commander Capt. Lorenzo Fessler called to report that he, too, was under attack from both sides of the road. Delta was behind Charlie in the order of march and still on the north side of stream 12. The heavy volume of fire meant that Delta could not cross the bridge; neither could they ford the canal without first eliminating the Viet Cong shooting at them. Fessler wanted to use fire and maneuver to get his men down along the canal to force a crossing and come to Charlie Company's aid. Henchman said no. He new from five months of experience fighting the Viet Cong in War Zone C that early commitment in the wrong place could be a tactical error that would limit his options and further endanger troops not yet committed.

He wanted to assess the size and disposition of the enemy force first. At the moment, there were just too many uncertainties. Where was the enemy set up? How many were there? He knew Charlie Company was in trouble, but he didn't want to make it worse by sending in Delta and getting them caught up in the same trap.

As Henchman set about trying to find out what was going on, A. M. Dean immediately jumped into his UH-1 command and control helicopter and got airborne. He managed to contact Charlie Company commander Willie Gore by radio and began calling in 105mm howitzer fire from the First Battalion, Eighth Field Artillery, which was providing indirect fire support for the Manchus.

Within five minutes, the noise rose to an even more intense level, as the 105s began slamming into targets on the right of the lead element where it seemed the initial firing had come from. Dean was soon putting the howitzers on the tree line to Charlie Company's west. From 2,000 feet above the battlefield the artillery officer adjusted fire, trying to get each thirty-three pound, high-explosive shell where it could do the maximum damage, but the artillery seemed to have no effect on the tempo of the attack. Dean himself became a target, and AK47 fire began pinging through the thin magnesium skin of his helicopter. The pilot could not tell how much damage had been done to the machine, so he brought the aircraft down on the road near

Henchman's command post to inspect it. Satisfied that whatever damage had been done was manageable, the pilot put Dean back in the air. By this time, however, the helicopter was low on fuel and had to return to Cu Chi some 20 miles distant to refuel.

Back at the head of the column Pfc. James Elliott was somehow still untouched even though he was lying in the open, totally exposed to the bursts of machine-gun fire raking the road. For some reason the Go Mon machine gunner was not shooting at him even though he lay in plain view. Looking for something to shoot at, Elliott opened fire on some bushes on the east side of the road where he thought the nearest Viet Cong machine gun might be. Almost instantly an RPG came streaking out of the woods to his right and exploded on the asphalt next to him, knocking him unconscious.

At about the same time, all up and down the road, on both sides, there were more explosions, as another coordinated series of blasts from claymore mines and RPGs tore through the men lying unprotected in the shallow depressions on the shoulders of the road. What had looked like the only possible shelter from the deadly machine-gun fire had turned into an even worse place to be. The Quyet Thang Regiment had planned the ambush with devastating effectiveness. They knew that those Americans not killed in the first seconds of machine-gun and automatic-rifle fire raking both sides of the column would instinctively dive for cover in the shallow depressions. When that happened the Viet

Cong would hit them with either command-detonated mines or RPGs. Some of the Americans took the full force of the explosions and were blown apart in the blasts. The ambush was now almost ten-minutes old, but for the men still alive it was far from over.

A rocket-propelled grenade, or RPG, is a shoulder-fired weapon that launches a warhead over a short distance. The warheads vary from high explosive, for use against such targets as bunkers, to anti-tank shells designed to penetrate the steel plating of tanks and other armored vehicles. The most common RPG used by the Go Man battalion was the RPG-2, a Russian design dating from World War II. It consists of a reusable launcher and the rocket-propelled grenades themselves. Its maximum range is only about 100 yards. The RPG-2 was commonly known as the B40 by the Manchus and was grudgingly admired for its simplicity and reliability. Its 2kg, 85mm, shaped-charge warhead and rocket motor is capable of penetrating up to 180mm of steel armor. When the Go Mon opened up with a rapid-fire succession of RPG shots, targeting the men they could see still moving on the roads and in the shallow ditches, Charlie Company commander Capt. Willie Gore's command group was one of the targets. First Platoon leader, sergeant Arthur Minjarez, saw the RPG score a direct hit on them.

Willie Gore was dazed from the blast. He looked in disbelief at his rifle. It had been cut completely in half. He didn't think he had been hit, but he couldn't tell for sure because for some reason he couldn't move his legs. Then he saw that two of his radio operators were lying across the lower part of his body. Both were dead. From his position, the company commander could see an enemy machine-gun position just twenty yards away among the fruit trees that lined the east side of the road. For some reason the machine-gun crew could not aim the weapon low enough to hit his body, though they tried. All they managed to do was to put six or eight bullets through the bed roll he carried on his back.

Nearby, Arthur Minjarez saw Gore throw out a yellow smoke grenade just as one of the Viet Cong nearby lobbed a grenade right on top of the Charlie Company commander. Minjarez tried to get up to help, but there was no way he could move from the shallow ditch. His weapon was jammed and useless. He was out of hand grenades. He had nothing to use to try to keep the Viet Cong's heads down so he could get to Gore and his group. All he could do was lie where he was and wait.

The intensity of the action made it clear that Charlie Company was in deep trouble. Delta Company couldn't come to their aid. Even Alpha and Bravo Companies, which were still at their night-defensive positions on either side of the road, said they had come under small-arms fire and could not move. It seemed to them that the Viet Cong had infiltrated during the night to positions close to the perimeters of the two companies but not close enough to have been detected

by the listening posts that both companies had sent
out. It seemed Alpha and Bravo Companies were
both pinned down. Until they had a better picture of
what was going on, where the firing was coming from,
where the enemy was, there was no way they were
going to be able to come to Charlie's defense, at least
not right away.

Battalion commander John Henchman's urgent
calls to Second Brigade headquarters that he needed
to be able to see what was going on yielded results,
and an OH-23 observation helicopter arrived to take
him above the battle. With limited communications
capability the OH-23 did not offer as good a platform
for coordinating all the supporting fires that
were at his command that the more capable UH-
1 command and control ship would have, but it was
better than nothing.

While the artillery was being controlled by the
airborne artillery liaison officer, Henchman was
briefing the commander of C Troop, Third of the
Seventeenth Cavalry, the helicopter gunships now on
station nearby but unable to attack while the artillery
was firing. Charlie Company commander Willie
Gore had lost contact with Henchman but was still
communicating with the artillery liaison officer Dean.
In addition to his request for fire along the wood line
west of the road, Gore was now asking for artillery
on the east side of the road where it seemed the fire
was even heavier. No sooner had the artillery batteries
begun firing on those targets than Gore was back on

the radio saying he urgently needed more artillery even closer, on the east side of the road. Dean feared that calling in 105s that close was too dangerous. Gore said, do it.

The 105mm howitzers were firing what the artillerymen call "danger close," where the risk to friendly troops may be as great as it is to the enemy. Bringing the fire in as close as Willie Gore wanted, the artillery commander began firing just one gun at a time, instead of the normal approach of using all six guns in the battery. The other battery with six of its 105 mm howitzers that was firing in support of the Manchus continued pounding into the wood line some 100 meters to the west of the road. Then, as the artillery began to pour onto the targets, Gore called in again, saying he had been hit.

It was the last communication with anyone from Charlie Company for the rest of the day. It was a little before 1000.

John Henchman's first look at what was going on 1,500 feet below was worse than he feared. It was a disaster. Gray-black smoke from the artillery and air strikes hung like a thick fog above the tree line to the east, and here and there small, dark-green clumps—the bodies of Henchman's dead and wounded Manchus—cluttered the road. Artillery, gunships, even tactical air in the form of F4 and F100 fighter-bombers were all still at his disposal, standing by to assist. Henchman had a pretty good idea where his men were, but aircraft and gun ships were limited in what they could accomplish due to the close proximity of Company D to Company C. He had ordered Company A and B to begin movement to "Channel 12" to flank Company C on the bridge, and was concerned that gun ships and jet pilots might mistake the movement of these two companies for enemy units. The situation was bad. He didn't want to make it worse by bringing in all that fire power on his own men.

Then the American advisor at an ARVN compound located several hundred meters south of the bridge, just outside the killing zone, reported that his South Vietnamese soldiers spotted what he described as four platoons of Viet Cong, perhaps eighty to one hundred men, moving rapidly north toward the ambush site. Henchman immediately shifted artillery fire to the south in an effort to block them and keep them from joining the attack. He also asked to have the ARVN unit to come and help take the pressure off Charlie Company. There was no response to his request.

From his position about fifty yards from the tail end of the right file Sgt. Frank Hettiger could see that all Americans on the left side of the road had been pinpointed and were methodically being shot. Hettiger could see Viet Cong moving through the wooded area to the left. He shot one as he darted between two trees. Then RPGs and grenades started raining down on the men lying on the left shoulder and the surface of the road. A few landed near him on the right side of the road where Hettiger, Sgt. Norman Prevo, and his RTO, Sp4c. Thomas Wynn, lay. Prevo yelled, "Grenade!" just seconds before the device exploded in the irrigation ditch beside the road, showering the men with water and grass. Then the Viet Cong began closing in from the left. Hettiger rolled three hand grenades across the road in their direction, to the place where he thought they might be hiding. He then began taking fire on his side of the road.

Hettiger struggled out of his heavy equipment and ducked under the water in the ditch, holding his breath as he swam to a small bush. He tried to work his way forward to where the company commander should have been, but he was drawing sniper fire as he tried to move along the ditch. Soon RPGs came crashing into the area around him. He crawled into a small clump of sugar cane, where he could still see the road but had some cover, albeit no protection. Then the artillery began coming in, hitting ahead of him and to the right, where the lead element was. The sergeant crawled back to the irrigation ditch and began moving forward again but immediately began drawing sniper fire from across the road. Hettiger crawled under a bush.

Ngueyn Ngoc Nham saw his first platoon leader go down. Second Lieutenant Nguyen Van Chieu had gotten up to reposition some of his men and get them spread farther to the west along the canal marking the northern boundary of the ambush killing zone. They could not afford to have any of the Americans get across the waterway, for they would roll up the flank of the Second Battalion ambushers and cut them off from their planned route of withdrawal. Chieu only managed to move a few steps before he was hit by a burst of automatic-weapons fire from one of the Americans who was still returning fire from inside the killing zone.

Dan McKinney could barely move. His arms and legs had stiffened as he lay in a pool of his own blood on the exposed surface of the road. Through the pain, he caught sight of something off in the small cemetery to the right. It was a Viet Cong soldier peering around a tombstone. Dan managed to raise his rifle and began shooting at the man behind the tombstone, but his M-16 kept jamming. As he paused to clear the stoppage, he looked up just briefly toward the Manchu in the file just behind him. He was just in time to see a bullet strike the man in the middle of his forehead, killing him instantly. McKinney somehow had succeeded in shedding his equipment and stacked it in front of him trying to make some sort of barrier between himself and the tree line on the left where he thought the worst of the fire was coming from. Then, somehow, someone was on his right side, a medic, and the medic was giving him a shot of morphine.

He began to relax, drifting in and out of consciousness. Then, he couldn't say how much later, he heard voices. "Finally, somebody is coming to our rescue," he thought. Maybe it was the morphine that made him too lethargic, or maybe it was a guardian angel, but McKinney decided not to call out for help. Had he done so he would almost certainly have been killed, for the voices he heard were speaking Vietnamese. Some of the ambushers had come out of their positions and were making their way up and down the road. He could hear men moaning, then gunshots and silence. McKinney was certain the Viet Cong were killing the wounded.

Rudolph Love heard the voices, too. He was as certain as McKinney that they were killer teams out finishing off those still alive. He and another man got out of the irrigation ditch they were in and headed north, trying to get away from the killer teams. They took cover behind a hootch where they found another man lying wounded.

Twenty-two-year-old Pfc. Marty Shoemaker hit the ground when he heard the first shots being fired. Unlike many of the other men of Charlie Company, the weapons-platoon member got a good look at the Go Mon ambushers. He saw at least two of them taking aim with their RPG rocket launcher. He immediately opened fire, but before he could assess whether he had hit his targets, a burst from an AK47 hit him. One round hit his helmet with a powerful whack, another tore into his left leg, and several others ricocheted off the asphalt road and lodged in his abdomen. The force of the hail of bullets that hit him, rolled him over. He found himself looking into the eyes of another man from Charlie Company. For an instant Shoemaker stared into his face. Then the man jerked once as a bullet struck him in the head. Shoemaker watched as the life faded from his eyes.

Sometime later a medic crawled up to Shoemaker and told him to keep cool. Then the medic was dead too, shot once through the head just like the other man. Shoemaker lay still, playing dead. He saw Viet Cong coming out on the road, shooting the wounded in the head and taking their weapons. He knew he would be next. He was not afraid.

He watched the killer teams move onto the road, heard the crack of their rifles as they shot the wounded. He heard someone near to him cry out as he was executed in the same methodical way. But the Viet Cong didn't shoot him. He was so covered with blood from the wounds to his head, leg and stomach maybe they thought he was already dead. [19]

As Sp4c. Charles McCamish swam back to consciousness, he became aware of a terrible pain in his right arm. He had only just started to return fire in the first seconds after the ambush was sprung, when the grenade had gotten him. Now he could see bones sticking through the flesh and knew it was a compound fracture. He heard helicopters and looked up to see one flying straight at him. Bullets hit him in the left arm and leg as the gunship raked the road with machine-gun fire. Despite these painful new wounds McCamish

19. The Associated Press, March 5, 1968

found the strength to get up and run straight down the road, away from the ambush and the gunships, screaming for a medic. He wasn't just going to lie there and let either the Viet Cong or the helicopters kill him. McCamish was with First Platoon, the second in the order of march. He ran more than 200 meters, nearly half the length of the killing zone, to try to get to safety. Somehow he made it.

The sense of relief that Denny Dubendorf and Leroy Williams experienced as they took refuge under the bridge didn't last long. Within minutes they were again under attack from small-arms fire from both directions up and down the northern bank of the canal. Every time they moved or tried to look around the I-beams of the bridge they drew fire. It seemed as though they were safe for the time being, but they couldn't be sure. Dubendorf tried to see if there was some way he could get a look at the road through the bridge structure. He managed to find a small gap that gave him a view of a part of the surface, and he was shocked to see that his platoon leader, Frank Tinkle, was still alive and crying out for help. Dubendorf had seen him go down and had been sure he was dead, for he had just dropped to the road, not moving, just *boom*, down like a sandbag dropped on the asphalt. But there he was now, crying out in pain. The lieutenant had suffered a number of wounds to his legs and was bleeding badly. There was no way Dubendorf could see how he or anyone else could get to Tinkle without exposing themselves to the machine guns and automatic rifles that were still sweeping the road. Running the gauntlet back they way he had come wasn't going to work either. Dubendorf and Williams had no choice. They stayed put.

Machine-gunner Sp4c Leonard Royston was a dozen yards ahead of Dubendorf on the right shoulder of the road, aiming his M-60 to the left, the direction that, to him, seemed to be where the nearest automatic-weapons fire was coming from. As soon as he did, he began taking fire from behind him to the right. He had to get off the road. And unlike nearly everyone else, he had cover nearby, a small canal that ran parallel for a bit to the main stream he had just crossed. Royston slid down into the small canal, turning to where he thought the shooter might be, when he heard a string of big explosions that he thought were command-detonated mines. He could not see across the road, but he thought the explosions were coming from the left side.

Royston found himself with three others from the tail end of the company. Before they had a chance to think, the Viet Cong began lobbing hand grenades at them from somewhere along the banks of the small irrigation ditch they were in. The canal Royston was in ran perpendicular to route 248 for a few yards before turning south to parallel the road. The four men had entered the canal in this parallel section and decided to try to move along the bend that led back to the road. The moment they made the turn they began receiving intense and accurate fire. There was a Viet

Cong position somewhere along the neighboring canal that paralleled the short perpendicular run of the ditch Royston was in. The group with Royston immediately moved back to its earlier position. But no sooner had they made it back than they were met with another shower of hand grenades from above, which wounded two of them. Royston was then shot by a sniper with a rifle as an RPG hit on the nearby road. The three wounded men were out of options. They lay in the irrigation ditch, knowing that every time they moved they would draw fire. Then the artillery, gun ships, and air strikes began all around. Napalm drops on the left side of the road were so close Royston could feel the heat on his face and the concussions sucking the air from his lungs. He, too, heard the Viet Cong talking as they periodically moved out to the road. He never saw them.

Andy Rodgers was still unable to move, unable to get any M-60 machine gun ammunition to Thomas Mork, who had to be running out of it. Then there was no need to try. The Viet Cong were out on the road, picking up abandoned weapons and shooting those still alive.

"Oh, my God! No!" Mork shouted as the Viet Cong took aim at him and fired.

Third Platoon rifleman James Elliott lay on the right side of the road near the very head of the column. He, too, was totally exposed. He was wondering which way

to go, what to do. The confusion of the ambush made
it impossible for him to say how long it had been going
on, but at some point the firing subsided, and Elliott
could hear someone speaking in Vietnamese. Elliot was
sure it was a killer team, although he couldn't see them
from his position. He sprayed the weeds and bushes in
the tree line with his M-16, and the talking stopped.
He then got up and sprinted to the left side of the road.
Unbelievable, what had to be the only bit of protection
along the whole damn road, and he had found it: a
civilian bunker. He ran past Third Platoon machine
gunner Sp4c. Virgil Cotton and riflemen Sp4c. Conley
Tillson. Both men followed Elliott into the bunker.
Pfc Lenny Alimenious soon joined them as did Sp4c.
James Rankin, the acting squad leader.

The men felt a measure of security as artillery,
gunships, and air strikes hit the area. Company
commander Willie Gore and his command group,
however, were lying out in the open on the left side
of the road, just a few meters north of the safety
of the bunker.

Augustine Lugo didn't know how much time had
passed since he had been hit, but when he came to,
he too, could hear someone talking. He decided to
play dead. Out of the corner of his eye he saw a group
of five or six enemy soldiers. He noticed that one of
them was a woman. The small group of Viet Cong
were walking among the bodies of the Manchus on the
road, taking equipment off the dead Americans and

firing back down the road toward the main body of Charlie Company.

Several of them came up to Lugo. One of them picked up his M-79 grenade launcher and the nearly full bag of high-explosive grenades. Two others rolled Lugo over, took off his web gear, and searched his pockets before rolling him back face down and hurrying off the road and back into concealment. Lugo lay there for what had to have been nearly half an hour, afraid to move. When the artillery started coming in he crawled off the side of the road and into a water-filled ditch and covered himself with palm leaves in case the Viet Cong came back.

Wayne Holloway lay half on, half off the right side of the road, trying to take cover behind a small bush no bigger than his head. He knew it provided no protection, but maybe it was giving him some sort of partial concealment, and that was something. As he lay there, time seemed to stand still. After what seemed a long time, but may have been only five or ten minutes, Holloway felt as well as heard the artillery starting to slam into the trees not more than twenty or thirty yards across the road. The shrapnel from the high explosives seemed to be flying everywhere. The concussion from the exploding shells sucked the air out of his lungs and caused ringing his ears. He began to pray.

Sometime after the first barrage lifted, Holloway could tell that something had changed. No one around him was firing back. He looked to his left. Alvin Cayson lay dead, surrounded by the empty shell casings from the dozens of M-79 rounds he had fired. Behind him, across the road, he could see a small group of men. They were dead, too. Holloway had never been more alone. He thought he might be the only man left alive and that if he was going to survive he would have to change his strategy. Stop fighting and play dead. Above all, don't move.

Manchu Battalion commander John Henchman ordered a pause in the artillery mission so that the gun ships could begin making passes on both sides of the road with rockets and 40mm cannons. After they had expended about half their ordnance, he again ordered a pause to assess the results. Delta Company commander Capt. Lorenzo Fessler reported that he felt the intensity of the enemy assault had subsided, although he was still receiving fire. Henchman ordered him to force his way across the canal and move to the relief of Charlie Company. At the same time, he ordered Alpha and Bravo to move south as Delta tried to cross the canal. Alpha would take up a position on the east of Delta, Bravo on the west. But as soon as Delta tried to cross the bridge, they came under intense fire from previously undetected positions lining the banks on the south side of the canal.

Alpha and Bravo company commanders also reported that they were still receiving fire, but both wanted to force a crossing some 300 meters east of the bridge and out flank the Viet Cong ambushers. Henchman refused, fearing that he did not have a clear enough idea of where the enemy was, especially in view of the fact that one of the F-100 pilots reported receiving small-arms fire area each time he made a low pass to drop napalm on the tree line in that area. This information led Henchman to believe that the bulk of the force that was attacking Charlie Company had moved to an assembly area just where Alpha and Bravo had wanted to attack. He most definitely did not want to try a forced crossing of the canal into what was likely the strength of the enemy force.

The intensity of the shooting seemed to have lessened somewhat. Now and again the steady roar of the battle would recede and the physical pressure on Denny Dubendorf's ears coming from the gunfire and explosions would ease. When it did and his hearing began to return, he became aware of other sounds coming from the bridge. It was like nothing he had ever experienced before, and for a moment he couldn't make out what it was. It was a mixture of a low, rumbling noise, almost as if something was causing the road itself to vibrate, along with some other sounds that together created a sort of high-pitched whine. Then he realized what it was: the wounded and the dying. At times it seemed only like murmuring. At times he could make out words. As he listened some voices would now and then become clear, and he could make out what they were saying. "Help me! Help me!" "Mama, oh Mama, Mama."

Then the fighting would come roaring back, and the voices would drown in the cracking, crashing sounds. The pounding of artillery and gunships, striking everything above him on the bridge and across the rice paddies to the tree line, would mask the voices. But the explosions were coming in waves now, and the pauses between them were getting longer. Each time the roar subsided, he would hear it again, even through his desensitized and battered ears: "Oh, oh, oh." "Mother, help me." Surely, they couldn't still be alive up there. Not with all the destruction raining down on the road, not after the machine guns and rifles and RPG's and artillery and gunships. Surely, their suffering would end. Surely.

Danny Luster knew he was still alive. He was not aware of being able to see much. He didn't know if it was because he couldn't really move his head and the only thing he could focus on was the featureless sky or if it was because the bullet wound to his head had damaged his vision somehow. He didn't know. He could hear though. He was sure of that. From time to time, he could hear leaves rustling somewhere on the side of the road. Was it the Viet Cong? Was some other Manchu still alive? He couldn't tell.

Luster could also smell. The odors of manure and rotting vegetation mixed with the sweet, metallic smell and taste of his own blood and reminded him of where he was: lying badly hurt on a road in Vietnam just a few miles north of Saigon.

Luster could think, too. He thought of home and his daughter, now almost two years old. But mostly he thought of his wife and what she had said when he had left for Vietnam. He couldn't get that out of his mind.

"Don't you come back to me less than a whole man," she had said. "Don't you come back to me less than whole."

Peter Condell and his First Squad of the Second Platoon had been assigned as rear security for the company. He was walking on the left side of the road when it started, just a little ahead of Dubendorf. Unlike elsewhere in the company, where the men first came under fire from the head of the column to the right, Condell first became aware of rapid single-shot fire from a carbine nearby, then, seconds later, a massive volume of automatic-weapons fire. As he hit the shoulder on the left side of the road, he saw an RPG score a direct hit on someone in the right file, blowing him to pieces. That blast was followed by more explosions: RPGs, mines, grenades. Another man, this time on his side of the road, lifted his head to try to pinpoint where the firing was coming from. The man's body just seemed to disintegrate when an RPG hit him squarely in the chest. Condell thought that the RPGs had to be coming from the left side of the road, but the rifle fire seemed like it was coming from everywhere.

Somehow Condell found himself surrounded by a small group of men who had survived the initial attack. Without speaking, they decided to try to make it to what looked like an abandoned hootch on the other side of the road. It was only a haphazard collection of sheet metal and mud with a straw thatch roof, but it was better than nothing. As the group ran, they scooped up a wounded man and dragged him toward the hootch. As they were about to enter, Condell fired into it to clear it and immediately received a burst of small-arms fire in return. The men scrambled back to the left side of the road where they again began drawing fire but, for some reason, were not being hit.

The wild confusion of the fight went on, each explosion becoming indistinguishable from the next. It was no longer just the guns and RPGs of the Go Mon battalions to worry about. Condell watched as, out of the chaos, a U.S. Air Force jet put a napalm canister down not more than thirty yards from where the temporary battalion command post had been set up on the north side of the bridge, well outside the killing zone.

Denny Dubendorf didn't know how long he had been under the bridge. He felt sick to his stomach, nauseous. Maybe it was the physical strain. Maybe there was only so much adrenaline a person could take, and when you went beyond that point you got sick. He didn't know. All he knew was that he could not leave his place under the bridge or the men who had followed him down the embankment would kill him. But he didn't want to stay where he was either, because of the voices. With each new lull in the fighting, he could hear them calling out,

over and over. Some of the voices were just moans of
pain. Some cried for their mothers. One voice, louder
and clearer than the others—maybe someone not
hurt quite so bad—was calling for water. Was it his
lieutenant? Frank Tinkle? He couldn't tell. With three
Viet Cong waiting for him just yards away in the grass
along the canal, there was no way Dubendorf could
move. He could not get to the wounded men, yet he
could not stay where he was, with his ears humming
with the pounding of the artillery and the voices. He
knew he was going to die, too, that those men who
had chased him would eventually find a way into his
hiding place and shoot him, too. He could not stand
the thought of suffering like those guys on the road.
He wouldn't do it. He would just end it. But Leroy
Williams was watching as Dubendorf turned the barrel
of his M-16 toward his own head. Williams reached
out, jerking the rifle from Dubendorf. "Not today,"
Williams said. "Not today."

Wayne Holloway lay still, not daring to move. All he
could see was the body of Alvin Cayson just ahead of
him in the file on the right side of the road. Just beyond
Cayson was another man. He looked like he was
dead, too. He wasn't moving. That was all Holloway
could see. He was desperate to look around him, to
check to the right where Chief Nelson had been, to
see if anyone else was still alive. But he was afraid to
move. He thought he might be able to if he just did
it slowly, in such a way as to draw no attention to

himself. He thought maybe if he moved his head really
slowly, the way he had done hunting squirrels back
home in Florida, it might work. Just a slow, steady,
imperceptible movement that would allow him to turn
his head completely to the right, back in the direction
he had come, back toward where Nelson had been.
He was afraid to try, but he wanted so desperately to
know if anyone else was alive, if maybe help might be
coming, if maybe there was some sign it was going to
be over. So he decided he would start to turn his head,
just like he had done hunting squirrels as a boy. It had
worked with the squirrels; maybe it would work with
the Viet Cong.

Then the artillery started coming in again. So close
that Holloway was sprayed with dirt. He could hear
the whine of shrapnel flying everywhere from the
artillery along with the explosions of Viet Cong RPGs
and hand grenades. He didn't know how long it had
been going on. It seemed like it would never stop.

Sometime later—he didn't really know if it had
been ten minutes or an hour or more—Holloway saw
someone moving on his side of the road. Someone else
was alive. It was a sergeant, a new guy just in from
Germany, and he was crawling slowly toward him. As
Holloway watched, he couldn't believe what he was
looking at: someone was out there on that road, still
alive and trying to move. Everything about the crawling
man was strange. It just didn't look right for someone
to be moving when the risk seemed enormous that all
that movement would get you would be a bullet. And,

in the bright sunshine, the dark green of the man's new fatigue jacket didn't seem right either; it seemed too garish and somehow out of place. Or maybe it was just that the man was moving. Maybe the man didn't understand what a terrible risk it was. He was new. But Holloway saw it clearly, anything moving, anything showing signs of life was being shot. Holloway tried not to breathe, tried to will his cramping muscles not to quiver as he lay still, watching the sergeant crawl. Surely, any of the Viet Cong ambushers could see the man moving, too. Was he crazy? Had he been shot in the head, or had he just snapped, lost his mind? It was insanity to move.

As the figure drew closer, Holloway became aware of the very pale, white skin on the crazy sergeant's arms. A new guy, not even enough time in country to get a tan, yet there he was, his white skin flashing in the bright sunlight and the garishly bright green of his new fatigues making him seem to stick out even more. Nothing could be more obvious to any eyes looking at that stretch of the road. Still, the crazy sergeant crawled, the toes of his new boots scuffing across the asphalt as he pulled himself past the other motionless bodies on the road. Surely he would be shot, yet he looked unhurt, and nothing was happening as he continued to crawl. Had the ambushers left? How long had it been since the ambush had begun? A few minutes? A few hours? The noise wasn't constant now. There were pauses when the artillery had stopped, when the jets and helicopters were not tearing up the tree lines.

Could Holloway start to move, too? He wasn't sure. Now the crazy sergeant was next to Cayson's body, not much more than an arm's length away from Holloway. His movement next to Alvin's still form had to draw the attention of a sniper if a sniper was still there. *Snap!* The man jerked. A pink and white hole appeared in a bare forearm. No blood at first, then a steady oozing puddle began to form on the asphalt. *Snap! Snap!* Alvin Cayson's body jerked as bullets aimed at the crawling sergeant tore at the dead man's clothes and spit up pieces of asphalt around the legs. Holloway called out in a loud whisper to the crazy sergeant but got no answer.

It was noon.

TEN

Relief

Once and for all the idea of glorious victories won by the glorious army must be wiped out. Neither side is glorious. On either side they're just frightened men messing their pants and they all want the same thing—not to lie under the earth, but to walk upon it—without crutches.

—Peter Weiss

Alpha and Bravo companies had moved from their night defensive position across the uncontested bridge spanning canal 11 to join up with Delta, which had managed to move to the northern bank of canal 12 near the rear elements of Charlie Company.

Delta Company commander Capt. Lorenzo Fessler had ordered his second platoon, under the command of 1st Lt. James Thomas, to move up on line at the canal while the second and third platoons on either flank laid down a base of suppressing fire. Thomas had maneuvered his men into position on the northern bank of the canal just west of the bridge. First Platoon then moved up on his right flank and started to cross to the east side of the bridge to take up a similar position. No sooner had the first squad crossed over the roadway on the approach to the bridge than they came under heavy attack by RPGs.

Fessler ordered Delta to pull back fifty meters so that gunships could be brought up to attack the positions where the RPGs were coming from.

Somehow in the confusion, the helicopter gunships from Charlie Horse, C Troop, Third of the Seventeenth Air Cavalry mistook Delta Company for the enemy. Thomas watched in disbelief as a Charlie Horse gunship launched a volley of rockets into Third Platoon. Five of the men were seriously injured. As the wounded were being tended, Thomas looked up and for a second time couldn't believe his eyes as an F-100 fighter bomber appeared above the tree tops behind the enemy, flying straight toward Third Platoon. Helpless, he watched as it released a napalm canister. The airplane was so low it seemed possible to hear the click as the napalm was dropped from its attach points under the wing, and the canister, almost as if in slow motion, tumbled end over end, straight toward the already battered and bleeding men of Third Platoon. Then fast forward, as the dull metallic tube wobbled over the heads of the Delta men and exploded behind them, the heat from its fireball, singeing their hair.

Thomas had been ordered to retrieve the wounded men from Charlie Company who were lying on the approach to bridge 12 as well as under it, but he told Fessler he couldn't move until somebody called off the gunships. When the helicopters withdrew, Delta began moving forward.

Sgt. Larry Criteser of Delta Company's weapons platoon and Sp4c. Keith Bolstad were among the first to get across the canal. Bolstad went across the bridge while Criteser went under it. Criteser, a non-swimmer, was worried he might drown. The water had been steadily rising all day, and he knew after a week of operations in the Hoc Mon area that there were places where it could be six-feet deep or more. With the weight of his gear and ammo, the only way to cross was to take a deep breath and walk submerged for several steps, until he came out the other side into shallower water. He was ready to risk it. But the tide had started to go out, and the water was not as deep as he feared, so he struggled through the water and mud to the firmer ground in the grassy bank on the other side. With security now set up there, Delta Company began sending men, one at a time, across the canal.

Peter Condell saw them coming. From their position on the opposite side of the waterway, he and the small group of men with him began laying down as much fire as they could to keep the enemy's heads down, if any were still in the area, and give Delta a chance to cross.

When the first Delta men came across, the enemy fire had slacked off, although as Condell and the Delta men began sweeping the area on the west side of the road, they were still receiving occasional small-arms fire. All along that side of the road Condell could see small depressions about five yards apart. The holes ran in a straight line along the side of the road. It seemed as though all the dead Manchus lay just a few yards away. Their bodies seemed almost to be lined up evenly in the file position they had been in when the ambush was triggered.

Lieutenant Thomas took his second platoon 200 meters south down the road through what remained of Charlie Company, then stopped on Fessler's order to wait for reinforcements from Alpha Company. By 1500 that afternoon the remainder of the Manchu Battalion had moved to within 100 meters of Charlie Company's lead element, where they set up defensive positions for the night and began recovering the dead.

As Delta Company moved, they expected the worst, and that is what they saw: a hand clutching a blood-stained family photo, another holding a miniature copy of the New Testament. Then there were the small groups of bodies, where it seemed that some had crawled together. Was it to treat a comrade, or was it just to be with a friend and not alone? It was not possible to say.

The distinctive whumping, clacking sound of helicopter rotor blades brought Dan McKinney to full consciousness. Instinctively he knew they were med-evac helicopters and that the wounded were being dusted off. He thought maybe he would be alright after all. Perhaps it was the lingering effects of the morphine, but he wasn't particularly worried when two of the dust-offs had come and gone and he was still lying unattended on the road.

Then he saw two men approaching. They weren't carrying weapons, and he knew from the aid bags they carried they were medics. He looked at them impassively. They glanced at him, knew he had to be dead, and began to move on looking for someone they might be able to help.

"Hey," McKinney said. "Hey." His collapsed lung kept him from shouting, but the call for help was loud enough, and they looked back.

The blood-caked clump was alive. The medics knelt beside him and began to treat his wounds. It was hard to know where to start. The realization that someone who looked as bad as McKinney could still be alive inspired them to look more closely at the bodies on the road. One turned to the motionless form lying next to McKinney. The aid bag identified him as a medic, one of their own, but it was too late for him. Ron Slane lay surrounded by the items he had pulled from his aid bag to work on McKinney.

One by one, as the other wounded heard the American voices, they began calling out for help.

Wayne Holloway heard the voices approach, and for the first time that day began to hope he might live. As his fellow Manchus from Delta Company came nearer, he tried to stand. It must have been at least six hours he had been laying there, in one position, willing himself not to move. Now it seemed every muscle in his body ached as he struggled to his feet and, for the first time, saw what had become of Charlie Company and his friends from weapons platoon.

It was hard to look at. But even more painful than the sight of the violent way so many of the bodies had been torn apart was the scene just across the road from where he had lain unable to move. There, in a small group, lay weapons-platoon medic Paul West and West's friend Larry Widener. Next to them lay Holloway's close friend Larry Walden. Had the medic been coming to Walden's aid, only to die in the effort? Holloway would never know.

Denny Dubendorf heard the sounds of running feet and shouted commands. He looked up through a space between the bridge and the roadway and saw Manchus running across the bridge. It was a squad from Delta Company coming to help.

He dropped down from his hiding place in the bridge to see a badly wounded guy from weapons platoon struggling to make his way back north across the canal as men from Delta Company shouted encouragement. Dubendorf took up a position facing the direction where the three Viet Cong who had pursued him had been, to try to provide protection for the wounded man if his pursuers were still there. There was no enemy fire.

The tide had begun to go out, and the wounded man was mired in gray-brown mud. The man's motivation to get out of the killing zone and across the canal to what seemed like safety overcame the pain from his wounds and the sucking, pulling mud. Eventually he scrambled high enough up the bank for two men from Delta Company to reach down and pull him up to the roadway.

Dubendorf and Williams made their way across the canal and climbed back up to the place where the road led up to the bridge. Looking north, back in the direction where the operation had begun almost five hours earlier, it was a normal scene: a narrow two-lane blacktop road arcing gradually to the southeast through the rice paddies, marshes, and jungle thickets of the Vietnamese coastal plain. On the southern side of the bridge was a scene he could not have even imagined. There were bodies everywhere. At regular intervals, maybe ten yards apart, Dubendorf looked at the bodies of his friends. All along the road, on each side, were dead Manchus, their bodies mutilated by RPGs, grenades, and bullets.

Dubendorf didn't know how to react. As the survivors began to rise one by one from their positions and start walking back toward the battalion command center and the aid station that battalion surgeon Capt. Larry Daubek had set up, Dubendorf broke out cheering, shouting, clapping, welcoming each survivor as he passed.

"Way to go man! You made it! Way to go!"

Maj. Raymond Massey, the battalion's new operations officer, noticed Dubendorf's behavior and went up to sit with him. In a soft voice, the major talked with the strung-out soldier in an effort to calm him down. Massey's quiet words helped. Dubendorf stopped the cheering, seemed to regain his composure, then turned to join the other survivors walking silently away from the killing zone.

All morning long John Henchman had struggled. He had first needed a clear picture of what was going on, but that had proved hard to do from the ground. He did not get the helicopter he had requested until an hour or more had elapsed from the time of the initial intense fire at the ambush site erupted. Once airborne he got a good picture of the battlefield and was able to direct artillery and air support.

He had needed the helicopter to coordinate the air support that was going to be vital to try to keep the attackers' heads down and off Charlie Company. He had also had the need to get the three other companies in his battalion in position to come to Charlie's support. It all had taken so much time. Most of the morning he had not been able to talk to anyone with Charlie Company, but he had been getting the artillery and air strikes in on what he thought were the best targets. He tried to keep the Second Brigade operations officer up to date with the situation but did not do it as frequently as he would have liked because he was busy with conducting artillery, gunships, and jets, and getting Company A and B moving across the water filled canals.

At 1315, even before the lead elements of Delta Company had made it across the bridge over canal 12, brigade commander Col. Raymond Miller was calling for a situation report and asking what Henchman's plans were to continue the attack. Henchman said he was still working on recovering Charlie Company.

Within the next hour Delta Company managed to cross the canal and started the process of finding the wounded and treating them. They reported back to Henchman that they had still not been able to locate all the elements of Charlie Company, although company commander Willie Gore had been found alive, but wounded, under a pile of bodies in a small depression on the side of the road. It was then that the brigade commander got tired of waiting for Henchman to give him an update on plans for continuing the attack. Colonel Miller radioed the Manchu commander and told him to meet at another location to discuss subsequent operations. It was the last thing that Henchman wanted to hear.

The death of Bill Roush, his operations officer, a week earlier, and the death and maiming of so many Manchus during the months he had led the battalion seemed now almost too much to bear. Worst of all was the scene before him. As his helicopter flew above the road he saw clearly, for the first time, all the bodies that he couldn't seem to get to. No one monitoring the battalion radio network could mistake the emotion in his voice on the open frequency as he reported the scene he saw and spoke of his "Manchus all over the road down there." John Henchman felt he had failed those he cared about most, and the brigade commander was ordering him away from his people just when their need for him was the greatest.

Henchman left to meet Colonel Miller. When he got to the location several miles away he saw the brigade commander was not alone. Miller was accompanied by the division commander, Maj. Gen. F. K. Mearns. Miller asked Henchman again what plans he had to continue the attack. Henchman was dumbfounded. Continue the attack? He had not even begun to account for the dead and wounded, had no clear idea where the enemy was or in what numbers, and Miller wanted him to continue the attack? The Manchu commander said he would worry about the attack when he had taken care of his men.

Miller turned to the commanding general and said Henchman had lost control and should be relieved. Mearns said, "You are relieved of your command. Who do you want to command until I get a new battalion CO out here?"

"There is no way you can relieve me now," Henchman protested. "Those are my people out there. They will expect me to come to their aid, not some stranger."

"Henchman," Mearns said curtly. "Get in my helicopter. Not another word."

John Henchmen felt utterly depleted. Mearns had a reputation for being one tough SOB, but when the two-star general's helicopter landed back at Twenty-fifth Division Headquarters in Cu Chi, Henchman found a patient, almost fatherly man. The commanding general wanted to know what had gone wrong. Henchman told him what he thought had happened. Mearns said he understood but given the circumstances, with that kind of disaster, he had no choice but to relieve him. Henchman knew he was right and suspected that had Mearns not relieved him, then Gen. William Westmoreland, the commander of all U.S. forces in Vietnam, would have relieved Mearns.[20]

20. Henchman, My Recollections.

Ambush survivors join with the rest of the battalion in recovering the
bodies of the dead.
Photo courtesy of Todd Dexter.

Heavy lifting Chinook helicopter of the 242nd Assault Support Helicopter
Company hauling off the personal equipment of Charlie Company's dead
and wounded. *Photo courtesy of Todd Dexter.*

Ronald Allen Slane
Slane was killed as he administered aid to the severely wounded Dan McKinney. McKinney credits Slane with saving his life.
Photo courtesy of Verna Slane.

Sp4c. Nicholas Cutinha
machine gunner from 1st Platoon, was posthumously awarded the Medal of Honor for his actions on March 2nd.
Photo courtesy of 4/9 Infantry Manchu (Vietnam) Association.

Pfc. Darrell Wheeler
the first Charlie Company casualty in the ambush.
Photo courtesy of 4/9 Infantry Manchu (Vietnam) Association.

Sp4c. Denny Dubendorf took refuge with Pfc. Leroy Anderson under the bridge spanning canal 12. The bridge in the photo is a more recent replacement of the original structure.
Photo by the author.

Sp4c. Thomas Mork
Third platoon machine gunner.
Photo courtesy of TheWall-USA.com.

Pfc. Clifford Stockton
killed in the first burst of machine
gun fire that also took the life of
Darrell Wheeler.
Photo courtesy of TheWall-USA.com.

ELEVEN

Aftermath

I'm gonna tell Mom we had some trouble but give her the impression it wasn't bad. So you'll keep it down. You might corner Preston sometime and tell him. Make sure he joins the Navy.

—Wayne Holloway, letter home, March 5, 1968

The Charlie Company survivors gathered together near the battalion command post, where an aid station had been set up. Dr. Larry Daubek, the battalion surgeon, quickly assessed the condition of the wounded, continued the treatment already begun by the line-company medics, and arranged evacuation of the most critically hurt. Captain Don Crowley, the battalion chaplain, was also there. Daubek set about treating wounds to the soldiers' bodies, and Crowley worked on the hurt to their souls.

Twenty-nine men from Charlie Company and

five from Delta required medical treatment. Forty-eight men were beyond help. Forty-six of those were from Charlie Company, and two others, Aristides Sosa and Larry Widener, were from Alpha Company Sixty-fifth Engineers. They had been attached to the Manchus throughout the Hoc Mon mission for the purpose of disposing of any rockets or other enemy weapons found.

Of the ninety-two men with Charlie Company who set out that morning, only fifteen were not injured, most of them were from the trailing elements of the company that had yet to cross into the killing zone of the ambush.

As Wayne Holloway sat among the small group of the survivors who had gathered near the makeshift battalion aid station, a lieutenant from Delta Company approached and asked Holloway to join him and a group he was getting together to "go after" the Viet Cong ambushers.

"If it's all the same to you, sir," Holloway said, "I believe I've had enough for today."

The lieutenant moved on, and no one set out to pursue the men who had destroyed Charlie Company.

Holloway and the rest of the survivors were then given the order to join with men from other Manchu companies to begin recovering the bodies of their dead comrades. They were helped by a company from the Wolfhounds of the Twenty-seventh Infantry Regiment, who had arrived that afternoon as reinforcements, after the action was over. Together they began gathering the dead and loading them onto a three-quarter ton truck that would take them to a collection point at the intersection where highway 248 met the road to the Phu Long bridge; there, the helicopter that had flown out the truck would load the bodies for the flight to the men from the Graves registration unit at Twenty-fifth Division Headquarters in Cu Chi who would begin preparing the bodies for shipment home.

None of the survivors had time to reflect on what had happened or to absorb the trauma of the events they had just gone through. They walked back into the killing zone they had wanted so desperately to get out of and began loading the bodies of their friends into the truck as it rolled slowly down the asphalt. In some cases, live grenades and other munitions had to be removed from the web gear of the dead to make them safe to carry. Some of the bodies were in pieces, so special care had to be taken to make sure no body parts were left behind.[21] Wayne Holloway and the others went about the work methodically, each man finding his own way to deal with the gruesome task. Some simply tried to put up a wall that would shut them off from their emotions and keep away the reality of what they were doing. For the most part it worked, but there were moments when the wall would start to crack.

Here, two severed hands, one black, one white, lay

21. One of the men of Bravo Company recovered a severed hand after the helicopter carrying the bodies had departed. At first uncertain of what to do he decided to bury it by the roadside. He dug a small hole, carefully laid the hand in it, covered it with dirt, and said a silent prayer.

on the asphalt, almost touching. It seemed symbolic of something, but Holloway couldn't say what.

There, the blood-soaked picture of a wife still clutched tightly in a lifeless hand. The man had lived at least long enough to have pulled the picture from the liner of his helmet. Those images were hard to look at, as were the faces of friends, but it had to be done. Maybe it was even better to have a friend do it. Wayne Holloway told himself they would have done the same for him if their places had been reversed. He owed it to them.

Denny Dubendorf was struggling with the same emotions as he helped load up the bodies. "How strange," he thought, when he came to his friend Red. Just the night before Red had managed to find some ice somewhere and had gotten hold of two cans of beer. In a trick learned from the little Vietnamese kids who sold cold drinks by the roadside, the two took their beer cans and spun them on the block of ice, cooling them down. Then they had sat together, sipping the beer, talking about the bad stretch they were going through, and speaking of how eager they were to get out of the Hoc Mon area. Red had been one of the lucky ones. He had just returned to the field from a few days off the line recovering from a shrapnel wound to his arm that he had suffered in one of the first brushes with the Go Mon battalions. Dubendorf remembered looking at the arm and noticing the stitches still hadn't been taken out and that the wound had that angry red look that made you wonder about infection. As Dubendorf reached down to gather up Red's body, he saw the arm with the shrapnel wound was gone.

Later that afternoon after most of the bodies had been recovered, the heavy-lifting Chinook helicopters of the 242nd Assault Support Helicopter Company, of the 269th Combat Aviation Battalion began removing the equipment of the dead and injured. Gerry Schooler, one of the Wolfhounds brought in to help provide security for the Manchus, found even that a hard scene to take in, despite being from another battalion and having known none of the dead personally. The image of the big helicopters lifting off with sling loads of personal equipment from the dead, suspended below, was one that haunted him. All that equipment, the web gear, canteens, ponchos, rucksacks with the extra socks, foot powder, toothbrushes and razors, paperback novels and letters from home, the odds and ends of everyday life brought home to him the terrible toll of the ambush in an unexpected way.

By nightfall, most, but not all, of the dead had been recovered. For security reasons it was decided that further searches be suspended and the remaining companies pulled back to a more defensible area outside the killing zone. They would continue the search for those still unaccounted for the next day.

Sometime later, when the last light was out of the sky, Nguyen Van Phi, intelligence officer for the Quyet Thang Regiment, made his way carefully out of his hiding place in the water-logged banks of the Saigon River to the edge of highway 248. Phi had been sent out to make an assessment of the situation, to find out, if he could, how effective the ambush had been, and also to get a sense of where the Americans were set up for the night. His senses alert to every sound, every smell, he carefully crawled along the side of a rice-paddy dike toward the pavement of highway 248. Then, heart in mouth, he crept slowly to the edge of the road. No sooner had he begun to peer down the stretch of asphalt than he jerked his head back into the weeds. "My God, I've crawled right into their camp," he thought, as he made out the forms of several men who at first seemed to be sleeping. His fright eased as he took in the rest of the scene: the clotted blood with its tell-tale sweet metallic smell, and the stillness. Phi could tell Lieutenant Nham and Major Tu Nhut that the Americans still had not recovered all their dead. As he slowly made his way back toward the river, he evaluated what he had seen. It didn't seem likely the Americans were in any shape to pursue the Quyet Thang the next day.

Charlie Company's survivors were pulled aside and excused from any additional duty that night. Someone had decided that they had been through enough. While the remaining three Manchu companies set up security, Charlie's survivors gathered together in the ruins of a small farm house. They would have no night-watch duties. The other men in the battalion would look after them.

Wayne Holloway lay on his back under a hole in the roof of the ruined farmhouse, watching a succession of illumination flares drift down through the darkness. A muffled pop followed by a metallic pinging announced the arrival of each flare, followed by the steady hiss of its luminescent fire. The gentle rocking of the flares as they swung beneath their parachutes caused the shadows to do the same, making the images jerk back and forth on the walls of the ruined house. As each flare burned out and the darkness returned, Holloway felt temporarily blinded, and the night seemed even blacker than before. It made him feel vulnerable.

Denny Dubendorf lay alone in another corner of the house, unable to turn off the sounds of the dying that were running through his head in an endless loop, trying to reconcile the conflict that had been his torment—of being so afraid of dying and wanting to die at the same time. He and Leroy Williams had become separated once Delta Company had finally crossed the bridge. When the two met a few hours later, Dubendorf had been surprised by the emotional impact he felt when he saw the young black man again. The two had embraced, Dubendorf collapsing in tears and sobbing out his thanks to Williams for intervening and keeping him from killing himself during the long hours they hid under the bridge listening to the cries of the wounded and dying above them. Now Dubendorf was feeling sick and cold. He'd lost his personal gear somehow, his clothes had not really dried after he had waded through the canal, and he had no poncho to wrap himself in. He was shivering and shaking until a friend, another survivor, came over to him and held him in his arms. It kept them both warm.

The next morning, the uninjured survivors of the Charlie Company ambush were flown back to the battalion base camp in Tay Ninh.

Dan McKinney underwent surgery at the Ninety-third Evacuation Hospital in Long Binh, Vietnam, later the night of March 2. A week later, on March 9, he was sent to Japan to continue his recovery. The initial medical assessment was that he would return to duty with Charlie Company once he had healed. But the wounds in his left leg were slow to mend, empty hospital beds were in short supply and he was still not fit enough to return to duty, so he was sent home. After recuperating for several months at the hospital at Ft. Leonard Wood, Missouri, McKinney was determined to be unfit for infantry duty and was sent to Ft. Carson, Colorado, where he finished his active-duty service as a clerk in a motor pool.

McKinney continued to have lingering effects from the wounds he suffered in the ambush, and in 1986 had major surgery to repair a problem caused by his initial treatment. A hole in the lining of his stomach that had not been repaired allowed a section of small intestine to become attached to his lung. He has experienced no further medical difficulties since, although the bullet fragment that caused his left lung to collapse remains lodged in his chest. Doctors have determined that the risk to remove it would outweigh any benefit from the surgery.

McKinney never spoke of his Vietnam experience, and as a result most of his friends, as well as co-workers at the company where he works selling trucks, knew nothing of what he had gone through until an independent filmmaker featured McKinney in the documentary "A Time For Honor," broadcast on PBS in 2003. He attended his first reunion of the Manchus in September 2000 and credits the experience as a plus in the healing process. He, his wife, and two daughters live in Effingham, Illinois.

Wayne Holloway had the bulk of his one-year Vietnam tour ahead of him. But, like most of the rest of the survivors, it was not in Charlie Company. The company was rebuilt with new replacements. Only those who specifically asked to remain in Charlie Company did so. Holloway's new assignment was with the battalion's heavy-weapons platoon, the 4.2 inch mortar unit. After his year was up, he returned to his native Florida, where he and his wife, Sharon, raised two sons. Of the seventeen men from weapons platoon who were split up among the rifle platoons for the operation the day of the ambush, ten died and four were wounded. He was one of three who escaped injury.

Denny Dubendorf finished his three-year enlistment with a tour of duty in the Second Infantry Division on the De-militarized-zone in Korea. On his return to civilian life, he went to work for a time building cars for Oldsmobile in Lansing, Michigan. He is now an ordained minister who has served in churches in

Michigan and Florida.

On March 3 Lt. Col. John Henchman returned to the battalion base camp in Tay Ninh to pack up his belongings and to meet with the survivors of the ambush and bid them an emotional farewell. Henchman had contacted a former boss from the Pentagon, told him he had been relieved of duty and asked for and was given the job of acting chief of staff of the First Logistics Command in Long Binh. He was promoted to colonel and retired after a twenty-eight-year army career that included additional tours at the Pentagon.

In 1977, as a senior officer at Fort Benning, Georgia, John Henchman was able to get a new infantry training barracks there named in honor of Major Bill Roush, who was posthumously awarded the Distinguished Service Cross, First Oak Leaf Cluster (second award of the medal) for his actions on February 26, 1968. Bill's widow, Gale, and his son, Wake, came to Ft. Benning from Houston for that event. An oil painting of Bill Roush and his two distinguished-service citations are on display there.

After recovering from his wounds, Charlie Company commander Capt. Willie Gore was reassigned as a company commander with the Seventh Cavalry Regiment of the First Cavalry Division. He retired from the U.S. Army at the rank of colonel after a twenty-nine-year career.

Sp4c. Danny Luster was hospitalized for nearly a year. He underwent multiple surgeries in attempts to repair the extensive damage done by the seven gunshot wounds and the RPG wound to his abdomen. He was medically retired from the army in 1970 and returned to civilian life. He suffers from chronic pain, has limited use of his right arm, and has never been able to work because of his injuries. His first marriage ended in divorce. He lives in Springfield, Missouri, with his second wife, two children, and two grandchildren.

Sp4c. Nicholas Cutinha of Alva, Florida, was posthumously awarded the Medal of Honor for his actions in the ambush. The citation reads,

> For conspicuous gallantry and intrepidity in action at the risk of his life above and beyond the call of duty — While serving as a machine gunner with Company C, Sp4c. Cutinha accompanied his unit on a combat mission near Gia Dinh. Suddenly his company came under small arms, automatic weapons, mortar and rocket propelled grenade fire, from a battalion size enemy unit. During the initial hostile attack, communication with the battalion was lost and the company commander and numerous members of the company became casualties. When Sp4c. Cutinha observed that his company was pinned down and disorganized, he moved to the front with complete disregard for his safety, firing his machinegun at the charging enemy. As he moved forward he drew fire on his own position and was seriously wounded in the

leg. As the hostile fire intensified and half of the company was killed or wounded, Sp4c. Cutinha assumed command of all the survivors in his area and initiated a withdrawal while providing covering fire for the evacuation of the wounded. He killed several enemy soldiers but sustained another leg wound when his machinegun was destroyed by incoming rounds. Undaunted, he crawled through a hail of enemy fire to an operable machinegun in order to continue the defense of his injured comrades who were being administered medical treatment. Sp4c. Cutinha maintained this position, refused assistance, and provided defensive fire for his comrades until he fell mortally wounded. He was solely responsible for killing 15 enemy soldiers while saving the lives of at least 9 members of his own unit. Sp4c. Cutinha's gallantry and extraordinary heroism were in keeping with the highest traditions of the military service and reflect great credit upon himself, his unit, and the U.S. Army.

Nicholas Cutinha was one of three Manchus to receive the nation's highest award for valor during the four-and-a-half years the battalion served in Vietnam. He is buried at Fort Denaud Cemetery, Fort Denaud, Florida.

Sp4c Ernest Rosado Sr. of Middletown, New York, survived the March 2nd ambush without injury, and asked to serve out the remaining four months of his tour with Charlie Company. He died in combat on May 5, 1968, six weeks short of his twenty-first birthday.

Pfc. Gazzett B. Brunson of Chicago, Illinois, survived the ambush without injury. He died in an accidental shooting on May 25, 1968. He had asked to serve the remaining seven months of his tour of duty in Vietnam with Charlie Company. He is buried at Oak Ridge Cemetery, Oak Ridge, Illinois.

Pfc. Larry R. Olson of McHenry, North Dakota, survived the ambush without injury but died in a firefight with Viet Cong forces in Binh Duong province on June 19, 1968, one week short of his twenty-third birthday.

On December 22, 1968, the men of the newly reconstituted Charlie Company, Fourth Battalion, Ninth Infantry fought a pitched battle with another large enemy force, this time the North Vietnamese Army regulars of the 207th Regiment of the People's Army of Vietnam. Seventeen Manchus died in the battle.[22] When it was over at dawn on the 23rd, after evacuating their wounded and the bodies of their comrades who died in the fight, the Manchus set about collecting the enemy dead for burial. As they

---

22. Dennis Dulebohn, Gary Everett, Willie James Tate, Alfred Viel, Terry J. Ward of B Company. Justin Anderson, Richard George Barnard, Donald George Bousley, Richard T Chambers, Donald Culshaw, Charles P. Glenn, Manuel D Madruga , Henry E. Maul, Michael Anthony Minko, Dioniso Sanchez-Ortiz, Ernest J. Stidham, Malcolm Roscoe True of C Company

policed up the area, they also assembled the weapons they found on the battlefield. One was a U.S.-issued M-79 grenade launcher with the same serial number as the weapon taken from Augustine Lugo by Go Mon guerrillas who had mistaken him for dead as he laid on highway 248.

Verna Slane does not remember much about the day she got the news of her son's death. She had been working at her photo shop in Lincoln City, Oregon, when a man in uniform walked in. At first she thought he might have some business to discuss, but the look on his face and the tone of his voice told her why he had come. About all she recalls of the notification was that she was not willing to accept what the soldier was telling her, that her son had been killed, and she began pounding on the man's chest with her fists, punishing him for the terrible pain he was inflicting on her with his news.

Verna Slane opposed the Vietnam War even while her son was serving, but she never accepted the argument of others with similar anti-war sentiments that those who died, died in vain. She has never displayed any of the medals awarded to Ron for his heroic acts trying to save his fellow Manchus. She says they do not mean too much to her. "Only that I know he did what he was supposed to do, what he was told to do, and did it well," she says. "And that's all they mean to me."

Sp5c. Ronald Allen Slane, conscientious objector, medic, and recipient of the Silver Star and Bronze Star with V (valor) for actions prior to the ambush on

March 2, 1968, whose last act on this earth was to ease
the suffering of his fellow Manchu Dan McKinney,
is buried at the Willamette National Cemetery in
Willamette, Oregon.

Two days after the ambush of Charlie Company, all but
twelve of the nearly 200 men of the First and Second
Go Mon Battalions were killed in an air strike, caught
in the open as they were forming up to attack the
South Vietnamese Army compound in the Hoc Mon
district. First Company commander Nguyen Ngoc
Nham was seriously injured in the air strike, suffering
shrapnel wounds to his abdomen and right leg. Viet
Cong medics working in an underground clinic not
far from the site of the March 2nd ambush repaired
most of the damage and were able to save his right
leg, although massive tissue loss in that limb meant
that he would forever walk with a limp. Two Go Mon
colleagues carried him by stretcher more than 200
miles to a Viet Cong sanctuary in Cambodia, where he
remained for two years recuperating from the wounds
and the field surgery. Nham returned to the Hoc Mon
area in mid-1970. For the remainder of the war he ran
a medical-aid station for the Quyet Thang Regiment in
the same area where he had commanded his company
of the Second Go Mon Battalion

Nguyen Van Phi continued to operate as the
intelligence officer of the second battalion after it
reconstituted. The organization had begun the slow
process of recruiting and training replacements but

was not yet back up to strength when it suffered serious losses in another encounter with U.S. forces near the city of Long Binh late in 1968. This time Phi was there. He was wounded seriously and captured. After a few months as a prisoner of war, he was given the opportunity to join the South Vietnamese Army and did so, spending his last three years fighting for the government he had fought against as a member of the Second Go Mon Battalion of the Quyet Thang Regiment.

During the four years and seven months of their service in Vietnam, the Fourth Battalion, Ninth Infantry (Manchu) recorded 428 dead. The first death occurred on April 15, 1966, the last on November 1, 1970. Exactly half of the deaths (214) were recorded by March 2, 1968. More than 4,000 Manchus are estimated to have been wounded. Although their experience of the ambush was unique among U.S. infantry units, the casualty figures were typical of a U.S. combat infantry battalion during American involvement in the war in Vietnam.[23]

23. Richard Coffelt Database of American Vietnam War Casualties.

TWELVE

Post Mortem

Everything seemed like it was well planned.

—Pfc. James Elliott, Charlie Company 4/9 Manchus, After Action Interview, Tay Ninh Base Camp, March 4, 1968

Two days after the ambush a memorandum was prepared on the orders of Col. Raymond O. Miller, commanding officer of the Second Brigade, Twenty-fifth Infantry Division, the brigade to which the Manchus had been temporarily assigned for the Hoc Mon operation. It went as follows.

> 1. General. On the morning of 2 March 1968, Company C of the 4th Battalion, 9th Infantry was the advance company in the Battalion's approach march moving south to an attack position on the road near Ap Dong Hung in the vicinity of XT845036. Company C had departed their night

location vicinity XT849043 at 0840 hours and proceeded down the road across two major canals when they were ambushed by an estimated VC Company at or about 0910 hours. D Company was immediately behind C Company and they were to be followed by A Company which was at that time in a security position along the road in the vicinity of the first canal. B Company was to the west of the road and had made light contact that morning and was not involved in the action of the day. The Battalion Commander was at his CP at the time of the ambush and he immediately was notified of the action by the C Company Commander. The battle lasted throughout the day and at or about 1530 hours the VC broke contact and elements of D Company were able to move into the ambush site and clear the area.

2. Situation. Captain Gore, the Commanding Officer of C Company, had received his order for the Reconnaissance in Force (RIF) mission for 2 March 1968 on the afternoon of 1 March 1968. Captain Gore's Company was to move out and lead the 4th Battalion, 9th Infantry south along the roadway and be in his attack position at 0915 and be prepared to cross the LD at 1000 hours. Company C had the southern portion of the Battalion AO, D Company

would be in the center and A Company would be on the north. The Battalion was to sweep the area to the west of the road and search out and destroy VC, rocket sites, bunkers, etc. Each company had been given detailed instructions as to zones of operation, objectives, coordination, etc.

A final meeting had been held at 0730 hours on the morning of 2 March 1968 with the Company Commanders and the S-3 where final coordination was made and discussion had been held on actions to be taken in case of contact during the day. At this meeting the S-3 and C Company Commander had estimated it would take 30 minutes for C Company to move from their night location to their attack position (approximately 1200 meters). Following this meeting the Company Commanders of C and D Companies flew a visual reconnaissance in an OH-23 along the approach march route to their attack positions, over the LD and checked their area of operations for the day. They returned by the same route. At 0840 hours C Company moved out south along the roadway. The men were in platoon column along each side of the road with 10 to 12 meters between men, 20 to 25 meters between platoons with a point of approximately 40 meters in front of the lead platoon. The order of march was 3rd Platoon,

Command Group, 1st Platoon followed by 2nd Platoon. Elements of the weapons platoon (MG and 90mm) were attached to each rifle platoon. As the company moved south along the road they passed through Company A whose night position was in that location and secured up to the first canal and bridge 11. Once across the first bridge, the Company was in an area that had not been occupied by friendly forces. As C Company moved south along the road between 1st and 2nd canal a number of Vietnamese were in the column moving south also. As they approached the 2nd canal (bridge 12) these Vietnamese were seen to stop and turn around and head back in a northern direction. A number of men reported at about this time seeing two or three Vietnamese approach the main road from side trails and then turn and move back in the direction from which they came. Several men reported they noticed some hand made signs tacked to road signs or stuck along the shoulders of the road as they neared the 2nd canal; one of these signs was in English and Vietnamese. "US officers and men! Demand an end to war, demand repatriation! Vietnam affairs must be settled by Vietnamese themselves!" These men stated that these signs were not there the day before since C Company had secured this same road at 1600 down to a position 350 meters south of the 2nd canal. Captain Gore stated that he felt relatively secure moving down the road since his company had out posted the road the day before and the fact that A Company had occupied a position up to the 1st canal with OP's out to the vicinity of the 2nd canal the night before without making any contact or report of movement. He also stated that he considered putting out flank security but that he was pushing his movement in order to reach his attack position on time and he estimated under the circumstances the flank security would delay him too long. Captain Gore also stated that he felt the PF outpost that was approximately 800 meters south of the 2nd canal offered additional security and the fact that he had flown over the route in an OH-23 without any sightings led him to believe the route was not hazardous. As the point of C Company reached a position approximately 300 meters south of the 2nd canal, the VC sprung the ambush by firing machine guns from the right side of the roadway near the point of the column. Almost immediately the entire column came under heavy fire automatic fire from both sides of the road with the heaviest fire coming from the right. The men of C Company that were not hit in this initial burst of fire dispersed

to each side of the road and began to
return fire.

Captain Gore quickly estimated that the
attack was coming from the right front of
his column and confirmed this with his lead
platoon and ordered his 2nd platoon to move
up to the left side of the road and to move
up to reinforce the lead platoon so as to gain
fire superiority over the VC. As the initial
volume of VC fire had caught the entire
column on the road, the men had just begun
to reorganize and bring fire on the enemy
when there was a drastic pause in the VC
volley and then a hail of RPG-2 and RPG-7
fire hit the entire column from the left side
of the road. This proved to be the killing
punch. The majority of the men had sought
this side of the road so as to gain cover from
the initial fire and lay exposed to their rear.
The VC had planned such a reaction and now
had the men of C Company in their zone.
As this extremely heavy fire was brought on
C Company all combat effectiveness as a unit
was lost, those surviving were reduced to
sporadic firing and individual acts of valor.
Captain Gore lost contact with his lead
platoon but was able to communicate with
the battalion for about 30 minutes. During
this time, he requested artillery support and
was in the process of calling it in when his

radio was hit. Staff Sergeant E-6 Minjarez who was the action Platoon Leader of the 1st platoon had initial contact with Captain Gore and received his order to move to the left side of the road and as he was carrying this order out when the heavy volume of RPG-2 and RPG-7 fire was received from that side causing heavy casualties and making it impossible to continue. SSG Minjarez returned to the right side of the road and remained in that general location for the remainder of the day. Sergeant Provo (*sic*), the 2nd Platoon Sergeant, was able to maintain contact with Captain Gore until the Captain's radio went out and then Sergeant Provo kept his radio on the Battalion net and kept them advised of the situation for the remainder of the day. Specialist Four Rankin was a lead man in the 3rd platoon and was behind the point man for the company and he stated that the initial burst of VC machine gun fire came from his right rear followed immediately by another machine gun at his left rear. During the initial fire he and the point man dispersed and began to bring fire on the VC. As the volume of fire built up they received fire from all directions but that the heaviest fire was coming from the right side of the road. A number of men near him were hit and several tried to run back toward the column but were cut down. Specialist Four Rankin stated that a lull in firing occurred and then a tremendous volume of RPG fire came from the left side reducing the effectiveness of the men of Company C. He stated he ran and crawled about 75 meters north along the roadway where he dragged a wounded man to a bunker on the left side of the road where they remained for the duration of the day. Sp4 Cotton [Cotton], a MG for the 3rd platoon said that the initial fire came from a VC MG to the right of the road as he tried to get his MG into operation the entire column came under heavy fire within minutes and following the volleys killer teams were on the road policing up weapons and ammo. SSG E-6 Hettiger, the company field First Sergeant, was near the position of Sergeant Provo and stated that the initial VC fire came from the right front of the column and built up down each side within seconds. Sergeant Hettiger stated this automatic fire continued for a minute or so, then a heavy volume of RPG and automatic fire came from the left side of the road. As these VC were brought under fire by men of Company C RPG's would slam into their positions. Sergeant Hettiger stated that the VC used a great many hand grenades and RPG's but in his opinion there were no Claymore or Chicom mines used against the column. He also stated he believed that killer teams were close to the road initially and moved on signal to police up weapons. It was reported by Sergeant Provo and Sergeant Hettiger that the fire from their right was from snipers and that they believed some of these were in the trees. An attempt by Sergeant Hettiger to link up with his CO was made but due to the enemy and friendly fire he was never able to reach that position. Sp4 Dubendorf was a squad leader in the 2nd platoon who had just crossed the bridge when the column came under fire. Sp4 Dubendorf continued to fight from this position for the remainder of the day. Sp4 Woodall was just approaching the bridge when he heard fire at the front of the company, within seconds he and his squad came under automatic rifle fire. Efforts to push across the bridge were not successful due to the volume of fire being received from both sides of the road. Sp4 Woodall remained in the vicinity of the bridge for the remainder of the day.

This memo, written by the brigade executive officer Lt Col. James R. Mason, reached the following conclusions.

1. That C Company was ambushed because they had no flank security.

2. That the Viet Cong had observed the habits of the 4th Battalion 9th Infantry and set up a deliberate ambush for a company when and if it moved south of the 2nd canal.

3. That the Vietnamese people moving along the roadway on 2 March 1968 detected the signs and knew that the VC were in ambush and avoided the area.

4. That the ambush consisted of approximately one VC Company well armed with machineguns, RPG-2s, RPG-7s and AKs.

5. That the ambush was well timed, planned and carried out taking advantage of the terrain, the element of surprise, the estimated reaction of US forces and the fact that a natural barrier hindered the reinforcement of the unit.

6. That undue delay was made at the Battalion level in fully understanding and reporting the situation.

7. That the use of the roadway had become so commonplace to the entire battalion that a sense of security had developed in its use.

8. That 80% of the casualties occurred within the first five minutes of the battle reducing any combat effectiveness of the unit.

9. That the survivors managed to stay alive

and fight off the VC until relieved was due to guts and shear (*sic*) valor.

10. That the VC could have completely annihilated the entire unit had the artillery and gunships not been on station.

The conclusions in the Mason report stand as the official record of the ambush. They were drawn from what was known of the tactical situation at the time, as well as from interviews conducted with some of the survivors. They are surprisingly accurate in painting a general picture of what happened but, in light of new information learned from the Viet Cong soldiers who were there, draw the wrong conclusion in suggesting that the ambush might have been prevented if flank security had been deployed.

Both Nguyen Van Phi, the intelligence officer of the Second Go Mon Battalion, and Nguyen Ngoc Nham, the commander of the First Company, Second Go Mon, point out that the tactics they routinely employed, as they did in the March 2nd ambush, were developed for the principle reason of protecting their troops from the indirect air support (artillery, air strikes, gunships) of the U.S. forces. This tactic had the added benefit of being able to defeat flank security. The attacking Viet Cong forces were too close to the Americans to be detected by flank security.

The report correctly states that the gunfire came from both sides of the road and included machine guns, automatic rifles, and RPGs. The report does not speculate as to the location of the enemy beyond that general description. The testimony from survivors about how far away the attackers were is conflicting at best and confusing at worst. Many of the men in the lead platoon (Third Platoon) thought the much of the heaviest fire was coming from a distant tree line some 75 to 100 yards to the west of the road. But the ambushers tell us that nearly all of their men were positioned immediately adjacent to the road, only in a few cases more than ten to fifteen yards from it.

Former Lieutenant Nham, as commander of First Company, Second Battalion, did not mention any deployment of ambushers in the First Battalion forces in the tree line some 75 to 100 yards from the road. He said the First Battalion men were on the other side of the road and were deployed, like his own company of Second Battalion, right up close to the Americans. His version of events cannot be considered the definitive description of the Viet Cong deployment; neither can it be discounted.

It is also at least possible that some men from the other battalion, the Third Go Mon Battalion, joined the ambush later. This would account for the report that several platoons of Viet Cong were moving toward the ambush that was radioed to Henchman by the American ARVN advisor. It is also possible that at least some of the elements from First Go Mon Battalion had been held in reserve outside the killing zone and that advance elements of it may have triggered the ambush by engaging the lead elements of Third Platoon from a distance. Once the Viet Cong on both sides of the road began firing, this reserve group could have moved in to join those who had been hiding on the very edges of the asphalt. If that were the case, flank security again would not have discovered the ambush.

To conclude that flank security would have foiled the ambush, as the official report does, cannot be supported by statements from the ambushers themselves. Also, any assessment of the terrain at the ambush site would lead to the conclusion that flank security would have had to be sent out far outside the positions taken up by the ambushers. The flanker would have been walking down a tree line that was in some places at least 100 yards away. Any flanker in that position would have been far beyond the enemy positions and extremely unlikely to have detected the trap.

In addition to the element of surprise that concealment close to the road provided, the great benefit to the ambushers was that being in so close gave them a good defense against the indirect fire support, artillery, air strikes, and gunships available to the Americans. The Go Mon ambushers assumed, correctly in this case, that an American commander would not call such fire directly on his own position, at least not initially. The Viet Cong knew that the closer they were to the Americans, the safer they would be from the artillery and air strikes they knew were sure to come. It is extremely unlikely that the initial artillery fire missions called in on the tree line to the east of the road inflicted any damage to the ambushing force. It is certain to have restricted their movements, but the Viet Cong ambushers reported no casualties from it.

Captain Gore's decision to bring in the artillery right on top of his company when he became aware of intense fire coming from the left side of the road would have been more effective had it been made fifteen minutes earlier when all of the ambushers were still in positions close to the road. But the close-in artillery fire came after the ambushers had already withdrawn the bulk of their force several hundred yards east and west of the ambush: First Go Mon Battalion moved to positions east of the tree line that had already been targeted; Second Go Mon Battalion moved to positions several hundred yards to the west of the ambush. The only attackers left near Charlie Company were those manning the positions on the southern bank of canal 12, where they remained to keep the other Americans cut off and unable to pursue their main force as it pulled back.

In fact, Nham says the only casualty suffered by his First Company, was a second lieutenant who was shot, most probably, by Sfc. Frank Hettiger. Nham says there were no other casualties in the Second Go Mon Battalion, but given that there are so few survivors of the unit, it is not possible to verify that claim. First Lieutenant James Thomas of Delta Company reported that several enemy bodies had been found in the area east of the road where his platoon fought its way across the canal; other survivors report finding no enemy dead. These conflicting reports may be attributed to several factors, chiefly that Nham's view of the ambush was limited to the area where he had his soldiers deployed.

Another statement in the official U.S. assessment of enemy casualties also raises questions about accuracy. The second brigade, which the Manchus were temporarily working with, puts the enemy losses initially at eighteen dead, but three sentences later increases that figure to twenty without explanation.

But most of Nham's account of the actions of the Quyet Thang Regiment corresponds very closely with that of the Charlie Company survivors. The plan for the ambush was simplicity itself. The force evenly divided on both sides of the road but staggered so that their positions did not face each other; a pre-arranged signal—a machine gun at the head of the ambush—triggered shooters on the west side of the road to open fire, to be followed one minute later by the battalion on the east side. Fifteen minutes after the ambush began, all of the main force withdrew to predetermined positions several hundred yards east and west of the ambush, where they remained until nightfall. The only elements left behind were those along the south face of the canal whose purpose was to delay the advance of American reinforcements sufficiently to allow their main elements to withdraw.

It is also important to note that while it was true that the Viet Cong were aware of the American movements, they were motivated to act by concerns that the Americans might interfere with their own operational

plans, not because they saw an opportunity. Their order
to carry out the ambush came first. They developed
their ambush plan accordingly. Nham said his
regimental commander, Tu Nhut, had been ordered to
attack the South Vietnamese Army Compound located
about one kilometer south of the ambush site. Nhut
had concluded that the Americans were on the way to
reinforce the ARVN and *that* prompted him to act, not
because he had seen the Americans in operation, their
repeated use of the hard surface road, and decided to
exploit that weakness.

It is also important to note that the assumption that
the ambushing force consisted of approximately one
Viet Cong company is wildly inaccurate. A Viet Cong
company would have meant a force of between thirty
and forty fighters. We now know from the accounts of
Phi and Nham that at least six Viet Cong companies,
with at least 200 men total, carried out the ambush. It
is possible that as many as 240 men were involved.

What the Mason report gets absolutely right is that
"the ambush was well timed, planned and carried out
taking advantage of the terrain, the element of surprise,
the estimated reaction of the US forces and the fact
that a natural barrier hindered the reinforcement
of the unit."

For nearly four decades, important details about
what took place have been unknown to anyone in
the U.S. military or to any of the survivors. In the
research for this book, the interviews with the Viet
Cong participants in the ambush have corroborated

many of the assumptions made by those Manchus who were there on how it was planned and carried out. Was Captain Gore to blame for the tragedy for deciding not to put out flank security? In the nearly four decades since the ambush, conventional wisdom has said he was. In light of the new information, that seems now unlikely. The terrain on the west side of the road would most likely have led 2d Lt James O'Laughlin of the leading Third Platoon to have sent his flanker out to the tree line, for having a flanker walk through the middle of the wide-open rice paddy would have served no purpose. Had a flanker been in the tree line, he still would have been unlikely to spot the ambushers. In fact, the men walking down the road were closer to the enemy, and they would have been the most likely to have seen the trap. A flanker on the left, or east, side of the road, might have been more likely to spot trouble, but that too is far from certain. The terrain there was different, with small fruit trees growing in a widely dispersed pattern with underlying grasses. It was in these grasses that the Viet Cong were hidden. A flanker would have had to step right on them to have seen them.

It seems most likely that little could have been done to avoid the ambush. About the only way it could have been avoided would have been to have taken a different route to the objectives for the day. Considering the battalion's location on March 1 and the objectives outlined for the next day, it would have been very time consuming, if not physically impossible, to have gotten troops to the objectives on foot in daylight using any other route. In hindsight, avoiding the area would have been the only way to avoid contact with the Viet Cong, but that was hardly the objective. The whole point of search-and-destroy missions—later euphemistically relabeled "reconnaissance in force" operations—was to find the enemy and kill him. Senior commanders were trying their best to find the Viet Cong and North Vietnamese troops in all of South Vietnam, and they wanted to find them in large numbers. This desire to find the enemy, engage him, and pursue him if he tried to escape is evident in the comments attributed to the second brigade commander just moments before asking the division commander that John Henchman be relieved of his command. Col. Raymond O. Miller had asked Henchman what plans he had to continue the attack against the Viet Cong force they had encountered. The after-action report commissioned by Colonel Miller concluded that Henchman had been too slow in making an accurate assessment of the size of the force he was facing and for not informing his superiors in a timely manner. Yet at the time he was relieved of his command, no reference was made to what a catastrophe had occurred or to the massive number of Manchu dead; indeed, Miller's words suggested he felt Henchman was not being aggressive enough. Henchman's genuine concern for his men and the personal sense of loss he felt for all those in his command who died that day may explain the high regard the men of Charlie Company still have for him and the warm welcome he receives at each of the reunions he has attended.

It is worth noting the honesty in the accounts the survivors gave of the ambush, with no hint of embellishment of the role each man played. The only inconsistencies encountered when trying to reconcile differences in their recollections were due either to fading memory or to the fact that each man's situation was unique. Each had his own view of what happened. Because of the design of the ambush, with Viet Cong positions staggered along both sides of the road, some men experienced the heaviest fire from the left side of the road, while others said the worst of it came from the right. During the ambush each man's world was reduced to the very small patch of ground where he had lain trapped, a patch perhaps no more than ten or twenty yards square. No one knew much about what was happening to the other men in the company, and certainly none of them had any overall picture of the ambush and how it was carried out until after the shooting had stopped.

Some of the survivors said that the men who survived the initial heavy blasts of machine-gun and automatic-weapons fire were then hit by a coordinated firing of command-detonated mines that had been placed at several locations on both sides of the road. In one after-action interview a member of Delta Company said he saw blast marks evenly space every five yards, clear evidence to him that claymore mines had been placed in the killing zone, then detonated on command when the survivors dove for cover on the sides of the road. Other witnesses from Delta Company and several of the survivors from Charlie Company said that no mines had been used and attributed the blast and shrapnel injuries to RPG fire. The only witness among the Viet Cong ambushers, Lt Nguyen Ngoc Nham, said his men had not deployed any claymore mines but that they had used more than a dozen RPGs during the ambush. He said he could not rule out the possibility that other companies of the First or Second Go Mon Battalions may have deployed claymores, but he was not aware that any mines had been used. It may never be possible to reconcile these different assessments.

Discrepancies also exist with regard to the assertion in the Mason after-action memo that the Viet Cong had been able to carry out extensive preparations at the ambush site, specifically that they had dug fighting positions and built bunkers from which to engage the Americans. Viet Cong commander Nham says he did not receive a briefing on the ambush plan from regimental commander Tu Nhut until 0400 and, given the distance of some seven or more kilometers they had to travel to get into position, it would seem that the Quyet Thang would not have had enough time to have built many such fortifications. Lieutenant Nham also mentioned that they knew the Americans' night defensive positions were only a short distance away, no more than 300 meters, and that they could not risk digging for fear the sounds of excavation would be heard. He said his men simply took up positions near the roadside, concealing themselves under the cover of bamboo leaves and other vegetation. Their plan relied chiefly on surprise. By catching the Americans off guard, they expected to be able to deliver such a heavy volume of fire that return fire would be difficult, if not impossible, and that the Americans would be unable to pinpoint where the threat was coming from. Thirty-six years after the ambush Burt Haugen of Bravo Company insisted he saw many small fighting positions that had been dug in the rice paddies. He was certain the ambushers, or at least some of them, had lain in wait in water-filled holes covered with vegetation. Haugen believes there would have been little noise from the digging since it was soft, soggy soil and that the digging would not have had to have been extensive at all, just enough to create shallow depressions a foot deep or even less.

All the survivors spoke of how much difficulty they had had in determining where the ambushers were. Many believed that some of the heaviest firing, at least initially, was coming from a tree line on the west side of the road, some 100 yards distant. Alvin Cayson and Wayne Holloway directed much of their effort in that direction during the early minutes of the ambush. Charlie Company commander Willie Gore also believed that to be the case and called for artillery to be placed on that tree line. Lieutenant Nham said there may have been a handful of men in the tree line but the majority were right up next to the Americans, in places just five to ten yards off the road, in no case more than twenty yards. If Nham's description is accurate, then it becomes clear why the initial heavy artillery, gunship runs, and air strikes on that area had little effect. It would have needed to have been much closer to Charlie Company. By the time Captain Gore called for danger-close artillery, nearly on top of his position, it was too late to be effective, as most of the ambushers had withdrawn several-hundred yards to positions along the Saigon River to the east and in the marshy, grassy region on the western side of the road. There were also conflicting accounts of how many Viet Cong died in the ambush. The second brigade's report said twenty enemy soldiers had been killed. The citation for the Medal of Honor awarded posthumously to Nicholas Cutinha said he was responsible for killing fifteen of the enemy. First Lieutenant James Thomas of Delta Company also spoke of finding a significant number of enemy bodies in the tree line on the west side of the road, although he did not state how many. Yet many of the soldiers from Delta Company who were the first to arrive on site after the enemy withdrew said they saw no enemy dead. Lieutenant Nham said his force lost only one man in the ambush, a second lieutenant in First Company, Second Go Mon battalion, whose body was never recovered. Nham insists that that was the sole casualty. It may never be possible to reconcile these differences.

The conclusion drawn in the immediate aftermath of the ambush was that the Charlie Company commander's failure to deploy flank security was to blame for the ambush or, at least, was the chief reason why the ambush was so successful. The consensus view was that had a man been sent out at the head of the formation some distance on either side of the road, the ambush would have been detected or triggered prematurely before the main body of the company had gotten inside the killing zone. That opinion was expressed by the commanding general of the Twenty-fifth Division, Maj. Gen. F. K. Mearns.

"There was a hell of a mistake made," Mearns said to reporters two days later. "I just couldn't understand why the company commander didn't have any flank and point security. This is the same unit and the same company commander who in mid-January had one of his platoons fight the best platoon action I've ever seen."

Mearns continued, "They had 33 men cut off by North Vietnamese. They killed 72 we could count. We had eight dead and 14 wounded."[24]

Mearns said he could only guess how the same group could have walked into the trap.

"I think they had a false sense of security."[25]

No one in the military, then or now, would disagree with the view that flank security is essential when

24. General Mearns statement cannot be verified by Manchu casualty figures compiled over a six-year period (1998–2004). Alpha Company had five killed on January 4, 1968. Bravo Company recorded six dead on January 5 and one dead on January 20. There was no record of any Charlie Company casualties in January of that year.
25. The Associated Press (3 March 1968)

any large unit is moving through an unsecured area. Whether the Charlie Company commander was confused about his location and assumed he was still in an area secured by two of the other companies in the battalion (Alpha and Bravo companies had set up night defensive positions on the east and west sides of the road at the southern end of the area where the battalion was deployed) is unclear. Gore's Charlie Company had already moved beyond them, however, when he passed through Delta Company, which had initially led the battalion due to Gore's late return from his helicopter reconnaissance mission. Whether he decided against sending out flankers because his company was only going a short distance before flanking to the right to begin its sweep is impossible to know. But even had flank security been deployed, it is still not possible to say the ambush would have been detected before the whole company had walked into it.

There is the very strong likelihood that any platoon leader looking at the terrain around him would have felt the place to send out flankers would have been to locations where they would not have detected the ambush. In any tactical situation, terrain often dictates such decisions. Given the wide-open fields on the west side of the road, it would have been quite likely that a flanker would have been sent to the tree line nearly 100 yards away to the west, while the orchards on the east side of the road, with their dense vegetation, would have called for the flanker to stay much closer to the road, although probably not close enough to see where the ambushers were actually lying in wait. Simply put, the Viet Cong were well concealed and not in a place where they would likely have been discovered by men walking on the flanks at the head of the formation.

Another puzzle that still cannot be explained is why, despite having a number of men from Charlie Company noticing the curious behavior of local villagers, how they abruptly turned and left the area, no one became suspicious enough to halt the column and investigate further. The platoon leader who would have seen it first, 2d. Lt James O'Laughlin, either did not notice the behavior of the civilians or dismissed it as unimportant. What can be said about Lt O'Laughlin's actions in the next few minutes is that had the men in Third Platoon, the lead platoon, followed his urgings and gotten back on their feet to assault right, perhaps some of them would have broken out of the killing zone of the ambush, the area where the Viet Cong concentrated their fire. But Third Platoon looked to the right, saw nothing but bare, open ground with no cover, and assuming the threat to be in that distant tree line 100 yards away, decided not to risk it. It now seems certain that the threat was much nearer, perhaps no more than ten or twenty yards. Had they moved that far, the Viet Cong would have had to redirect their fire out of the killing zone and thus raising the possibility that the Go Mon ambushers would have exposed themselves and become vulnerable to a flanking attack by Charlie Company. It is impossible to know what might have happened had the lieutenant been successful in getting his men up and moving, but it is a possibility that has to at least be considered.

None of the information about the disposition of the enemy force was available to U.S. commanders until now, so it is not surprising that the conclusion was drawn that the ambush was the result of a lack of flank security.

It is a truism that in the military, authority can be delegated but responsibility cannot, and that is why battalion commander John Henchman was relieved of his command and has borne the blame for the disaster that befell Charlie Company. It matters little that Henchman had a battalion standard-operating procedure stating that flank security was always to be deployed. The fact that Gore did not follow the procedure does not absolve Henchman of the responsibility for what happened.

But hindsight shows very clearly that while it may have been wrong not to have deployed flank security, it seems most unlikely that it would have made any difference. Some of those there that day have said they felt unprepared for the conditions they were going to meet in the Hoc Mon area and that therefore some of the blame should go to Henchman's superiors who decided to pull the Manchus out of one area with one set of unique characteristics and drop them into a new, unfamiliar place with a whole set of new circumstances.

With the new information now available it seems clear that what happened on that road north of Saigon on March 2, 1968 had little to do with the failings of the Manchus. The conclusion that the lack of flank security was responsible was an easy answer for a military leadership coming under increasing criticism at home for its handling of the war. Pronouncements from senior officials, including Twenty-fifth Division commander Maj. Gen. F. K. Mearns, that a junior officer, Charlie Company commander Willie Gore, had made a major mistake create the impression that senior military commanders did not want to admit that an insurgent force was capable of carrying out the kind of well-planned and coordinated attack that was done that day. To admit the Viet Cong still had such military capability, so soon after the disastrous Tet Offensive would have been a public-relations nightmare for the Pentagon. The question, then, must be raised of whether that willingness to quickly dismiss as a military blunder an enemy action that, like Tet, was so successful was because it showed that the Viet Cong were nowhere near being defeated.

After three years of a steadily escalating U.S. military presence that put nearly 500,000 U.S. military personnel on the ground, such a catastrophe seemed to contradict Pentagon statements that the fighting forces of the Viet Cong and their North Vietnamese comrades were near collapse and that there was light at the end of the tunnel. The military's position that the disaster was the result of the failure of a company commander to follow accepted procedures and put out point and flank security was accepted by the news media in accounts published in the days after the ambush. An Associated Press (AP) story by AP Photographer Al Chang was headlined "Lax Security Brought Disaster."[26] Then there was the above-mentioned AP story, printed on March 5, 1968, in which Maj. Gen. Mearns expressed his astonishment that Captain Willie Gore had not had any flank or point security.[27] The *New York Times* also reported the ambush, calling it one of the worst of the war, but stopped short of placing blame.[28]

The survivors of the Quyet Thang Regiment considered the March 2 ambush their greatest victory in what they call the American War. Nguyen Dinh Vanh, the assistant company commander of one of the Second Go Mon Battalion companies, was awarded the American Killer Hero medal, the highest award for valor given to the Viet Cong. Lieutenant Nham was also awarded the medal. The Viet Cong tried to capitalize on the success of the ambush with their own account, which was carried by their own Liberation News Agency and was quoted extensively in a dispatch by the Hanoi correspondent for the French News Agency, Jean-Francois Le Mauff, who wrote,

> In the pale dawn light of March 2 a battalion of American troops marched along a road just 10 miles north of Saigon. They were heading straight into a Viet Cong ambush. The Viet

26. Al Chang, The Associated Press (3 March 1968).
27. The Associated Press (5 March 1968)
28. New York Times, 1968

Cong claims it wiped out the fourth battalion of the first brigade of the 25th division. Five hundred Americans killed or wounded, the Viet Cong says. The US command in Saigon has admitted to only 48 (and 26 wounded, with 12 missing). Whatever the actual numbers were, the battalion fell into one of the most murderous traps ever set in the bloody Vietnam War. This is the way the Viet Cong's Liberation News Agency describes the massacre.

The place was Quoi Xuan, a little village on Route 13. Close by is a bridge crossing a river that winds its way through rice paddies. The Viet Cong began their stake-out during the night. They were wearing camouflage that was so good even their commander could not see them from the road in the early morning light.

Soon American troops would pass by. The Viet Cong were attacking points all around Saigon, including Tan Son Nhut Airport. The Americans had to get rid of the attackers. The Viet Cong waited in their ambush position. It was 8 a.m.[29] Well before the Americans got to that little bridge the Viet Cong knew they were on the way.

29. The Viet Cong and North Vietnamese Army used Hanoi time, which is one hour earlier than Saigon time.

The Viet Cong commander followed their
progress along the road, receiving telephone
reports[30] from men stationed further south
along Route 13.[31]

At 8:10 a.m. the first American soldier
began crossing the bridge. Marching in
a double column, the advance guard of US
troops crossed the bridge and reached the
ambush point. The Americans were about
50 yards away from the Viet Cong machine
guns. That was where they stopped, reaching
for cigarettes, chewing gum, waiting for
the second half of the battalion to join
them.[32] The Viet Cong waited too. Five
minutes later, 8:15 a.m., a second company
of men, marching in double column, reached
the bridge, crossed it, and joined the advance
guard. That was when Hell broke loose. Viet
Cong machine gun fire raked across the ranks
of Americans, the heavy bullets cutting them
down before they had time to react. A few of
the US soldiers scrambled toward a small flat-
roofed house off the road, trying to escape the
hail of gun fire. But only to fall into a second

---

30. None of the surviving Viet Cong agreed with this statement. There
was very little communication between the ambushers, who followed a
pre-arranged plan.
31. The ambush occurred on route 248, not route 13
32. Delta Company stopped just short of the killing zone of the ambush,
while Charlie Company passed through.

trap, for a detachment of Viet Cong were already there, waiting for them.[33]

It took just eight minutes to wipe out those first two companies of the Fourth Battalion, according to the Liberation News Agency. A third company of Americans who had escaped the deadly ambush had called up air support. US helicopters and reconnaissance planes came swooping in, trying to thrust back the Viet Cong and give the American troops breathing space to pull back down Route 13.

The Viet Cong Agency claims two US helicopters were shot down. Jet planes followed up the first air action, but effective intervention was impossible. Their comrades on the ground were in hand to hand combat with the Viet Cong. Another group of Americans who had remained back near the bridge moved up to attack. But the Viet Cong thrust them back, pushing them under heavy gun fire into the rice paddies.

The rice fields are open and clear, but they were no better than blind alleys for the US troops. Weighed down by their heavy equipment, the Americans were unable to make headway in the muddy

---

33. Sp4c. Peter Condell had tried to lead a small group into the structure.

paddies.[34] They became target practice for
the Viet Cong. It was 11 a.m. The fighting
had stopped. The scene close by the bridge
near Quoi Xuan was as tranquil as it had
been three hours earlier, except for the strewn
bodies of soldiers from the Fourth Battalion,
the First Brigade of the 25th Division, United
States Army.[35]

---

34. The men had been moving down the road. Only a few would have
been in the water-filled paddies.
35. It seems the Viet Cong knew who they were fighting, although the
unit designation is incomplete.

THIRTEEN

Home

Do not fear your enemies. The worst they can do is kill you. Do not fear friends. At worst they may betray you. Fear those who do not care; they neither kill nor betray, but betrayal and murder exist because of their silent consent.

—Bruno Jasienski

Those members of Charlie Company who survived the March 2nd ambush did not know what to expect when their tours of duty in Vietnam ended and they returned home. Somehow, despite having been away from home for so long and quite out of touch, they knew that something had changed while they were gone. Mainstream magazines like *Time*, *Life*, and *Newsweek* had shifted their positions and were now criticizing the war policy of the Administration of President

Lyndon Johnson. Famous personalities like respected television newsman Walter Cronkite had told their fellow Americans that there was no light at the end of the tunnel and that the war in Vietnam did not seem winnable or worth the cost. Opposition to the war, especially among draft-age students, led to massive protests on college campuses across the country. These feelings grew into a wholesale condemnation of the war and, in a larger way, of much that their parents had valued. These anti-war sentiments led to a logic that said that unless one had the desire to bring down the corrupt institutions and leaders who had led the country into an unjust war, then one should be viewed with suspicion. The popular sentiment of the time was anyone not actively trying to end the war was guilty of perpetuating it: if you are not part of the solution, you are part of the problem. Anyone so much a part of the establishment as a soldier was clearly part of the problem in their eyes.

Somehow the Charlie Company survivors came home knowing that things had changed. They sensed that people felt differently about them than they had before they shipped out for Vietnam. Rather than expressions of admiration or gratitude for the service these young men had performed, the people at home were, at best, indifferent to them and all they had gone through or, at worst, hostile toward them for having fought. How these survivors of the March 2nd ambush got that sense of estrangement from the society that had sent them to war is hard to know. It certainly wasn't from the sanitized news broadcast on Armed Forces Vietnam (AFVN) radio. They knew that *Stars and Stripes*, the newspaper for America's fighting man, was no better than PAVN when it came to accurately reporting events having to do with the fighting. According to the paper the U.S. military never seemed to be suffering any setbacks, even tough battles being recounted as lopsided American wins. Stars and Stripes lost what little bit of credibility it may have had when it carried accounts of military activity in Vietnam the week that ended March 2, 1968 and characterized American losses as "light to moderate." It sure hadn't felt that way to the Manchus.

So the media available to them wouldn't seem to have been likely sources of the news that attitudes had changed. Letters from friends and family may have been responsible for the Charlie Company survivors' growing awareness that things were going to be different when they got home. No one stepping off the plane expected to be met by any welcoming committee other than their own immediate family and friends, and that was only if they were lucky enough to be from a town close to Oakland, California, where they arrived. Most simply checked in with the army-personnel section at the Oakland terminal, had their paperwork processed for leave if they were going on to another military assignment, or were out-processed if their active duty commitment was over. The next step was to get to the nearest airport and take a commercial flight back home.

Walking into that airport, some of the men felt apprehensive, unsure of how they would be received. Some sensed hostility, whether intended or not, in the stares of the civilians they met. While a few were greeted with expressions of appreciation for their service, most were ignored, just some more G.I.s lugging duffle bags through the airport. It was surprising, that sense of being ignored, for guys who had spent the last year waking up each morning wondering if that day was going to be their last. Just the sight of a civilian in the middle of some routine daily task could be a shock. There was something about knowing that while they had been greeting the dawning of each new day with anxiety, dreading what might come, the grocery-store clerk had been restocking the toilet paper and bagging the groceries just like always. Every day they had been gone, every moment that to them had seemed to crawl by as they held their breath, had been just another day for most everybody back home. Sure, their families had been on pins and needles the whole time. But college students had been getting drunk and dating girls and cramming for exams and planning for their future, while they had been dreaming of just one slice of warm pizza or hoping for what seemed at times like the million-in-one chance that they would be able to look again into the face of someone they loved. Few had been ready for the shock of realizing that the normal routine of everyday life had gone on for nearly everybody else, as though the war didn't exist.

Then there was the problem of talking about the

war to the folks at home. Most soldiers expected that
at some point, someone, a friend or family member,
might ask what it had been like. They were expecting
something like that, and it was one of the things
they talked about most during their time in the field.
Sometimes in the evening, a group would gather to
talk about just that. "What are you gonna tell them
when they ask what it was like?" Nobody had a good
answer for it. Words didn't seem to be enough. Could
they say, "There was this guy I knew and got to like real
well. We were both due to get discharged right after we
got back home, and we were gonna buy a car and travel
the country together. But he's dead now. One minute
he was walking ahead of me along this rice-paddy dike.
It was hot, real hot. We were all soaked with sweat. He
had a leech stuck on the back of his neck, peeking out
from under his shirt collar, and I was going to tell him
about it next time we stopped to take a break, but I was
tired, like always, and I wasn't thinking about anything
other than carrying all that stuff, that heavy, heavy
stuff and wanting to have Vietnam done with and over
and get home again, and then he was dead. Shot right
through the head. In mid-stride he dropped to his butt
on the dike and fell over sideways, didn't cry out, didn't
say a word, just died."

They couldn't say anything like that. It wouldn't
mean anything. How could they explain it to someone
who hadn't been there? They couldn't simply say, "We
walked across this bridge one hot and sunny morning
and then, without any warning, all Hell broke loose." It

wouldn't mean anything even though it had seemed like
Hell and it had seemed like everything had come apart,
that there was nothing real connected to anything, that
they were just in the presence of some vicious, violent,
totally uncaring machine, that they had fallen into
some indifferent metallic monster like the corn picker
at home that had ripped off that farmer's arm, only this
machine was so big the whole world had seemed like
it had fallen into it. But that wouldn't mean anything.
Words couldn't express that. How could they explain
when words couldn't express what it means to be so
afraid you have lost the sense of your own body? Or that
in the middle of a fire-fight a guy might find himself
suddenly looking at his surroundings and wondering
how he got there, how he had made it across that big
open field and done something someone who didn't
know better would call heroic but really wasn't. Words
couldn't say how disappointed a guy could be when
he learned that there is no real answer to the question
he had asked his whole life before all this started, "Am
I a coward?" Disappointed to know that he was and
wasn't, and sad, or even angry, in the knowledge that
the question had never really needed to be answered,
or even asked.

How could a guy ever tell them about the ambush?
How? The explanation, the detail of what happened
would be like an attack itself, piling indignity on top
of indignity on a caring person who could never have
been prepared for the truth of it. How could anyone
inflict that on someone else, especially his own family

members and friends?

And so, maybe, they were glad that few people seemed to ask. Considerate of not wanting to bring up unpleasant memories, friends and family may have just avoided talking about it. Their avoidance of the subject, their unwillingness to bring up the war gradually morphed into a belief that it wasn't them who didn't ask but that it was the guy from Charlie Company who didn't want to talk. And if friends did ask and the survivor began to answer and began to see the discomfort on their faces, then he knew he had crossed the line and had done what he said he wouldn't, and then he really didn't want to talk about it, to dump all that on them, to talk in such stark ways about the violence and brutality and senselessness of it. No one would want to unload all that on someone else, especially when it was so far out of the bounds of normal experience that it all sounded phony and made up and just another war story.

Danny Luster found that out the hard way. After long months of recovery from the wounds to his body caused by the bullets and the RPG and the wounds to his spirit caused by the disintegration of his marriage to a wife who could not accept him "less than whole," Luster found himself at the beach. It was a pleasant early summer's day, and the warm sun on his body felt therapeutic. Luster was adapting to his new reality and feeling positive about the progress he had made in recovering from the wounds and in his success at having convinced doctors not to amputate his shattered right arm, to give him more time to try to make it respond. He was learning to live with the pain they told him would be his forever. But Luster did not look like a winner to a three-year-old boy playing with his mother on the beach. The boy could only stare. The angry red welts on Luster's scarred body were like nothing the boy had ever seen, and they drew him like a magnet. He couldn't stop staring. The boy's embarrassed mother apologized for the intrusion, explaining he was only a child and didn't really understand what he was saying with his comments, like, "Look at that man, Mom. He looks like a monster." Luster assured her he was not offended and said he understood why the boy might be so curious and that he would try to explain. But the more he spoke the less the boy seemed to understand about war and wounds and the more troubled the mother seemed to become. None of it was working. The boy couldn't understand, and the mother just seemed so uncomfortable. Finally, Luster stopped. Once again he said that the boy's stares were no problem, then pulled on his shirt. He couldn't explain anything to the boy or to his mother. He felt he was only dumping it on them, forcing them to share in his pain, and what right did he have to do that. The incident bothered him. It bothered him so much that from that day on he never let any of his wounds show, not to strangers, not to family. The two daughters he had with his second wife never once saw the scars. Luster felt it wouldn't be right to make them suffer from his trying to explain his wounds, how he was hurt, and what it had been like.

He thought it was better to keep it to himself.

And, as other survivors of the ambush felt, who would want to talk about any of it when the guy telling knew as surely as he knew anything that his just being here, now, is all the evidence anyone would ever need to know his guilt? Why isn't he dead? What was so special about him? How could life be so unfair that all the others died and he lived? The others didn't deserve death, and he doesn't deserve the life he's been given. Why didn't he do his part? He could have gotten that extra ammo up to Porky so that he wouldn't have had to move out of his concealment to find another gun with a belt in it, one that was loaded and still worked. And then maybe Porky wouldn't have been shot again, and again, and again, until the bottom half of his leg was just shot off even while he lay there still shooting, still doing his job trying to save others. He, the survivor, could have done more. He could have done something. And now the others are dead and he isn't and he'll just have to live with that because he could have done more. At least he could have died.

What good would it do to talk about that? Nobody really wants to know, and who needs to tell them? What needs to be done is for everyone to just accept it, accept it and move on. What's past is past, and nothing anybody does or says can do anything to bring any of those guys back. Besides, the whole issue of the war is just too divisive. A veteran's father may have supported him, may have said to others that if they didn't support the war, then they were not supporting the men America had sent there to fight it. He may have even had a bumper sticker: "America. Love it or Leave it." Or maybe he had a father who loved his son and hated what his boy had been made to do. He may have burned with rage at the policy makers, the Greatest Generation, who decided it was all worth 58,000 American lives. But maybe he didn't know how his son felt about it all and didn't want to risk his son thinking he didn't love him. Does anyone really want to open that can of worms?

And oh, by the way, people at work and at school don't seem to want to talk about what that experience was like either. "They" were the ones who had sent him there, required him to go because "they" thought, at first anyway, it was the right thing to do. When it all started, he just knew he couldn't let them down. They expected him to serve, to overcome his fears, to be the man he was afraid he wasn't. And they were the ones who said it was alright to go against everything he had ever been taught and felt about it being wrong to kill. They had said that if he was a soldier, then he must do it, and it will be right because it is an unfortunate but necessary part of war. But now it seemed as if "they" weren't so sure that it had been the right thing to do and that maybe it wasn't really necessary after all. And he may have begun to wonder why he felt like he had been left holding the bag. That it had become so much harder to carry the weight of the killing that had been necessary when maybe "they" weren't so sure if it really had been necessary after all. They also told him to forget about that: We don't really want to talk about it. Why would anyone want to bring "that" up anyway? The war is over. Move on.

Nguyen Dinh Vanh
deputy commander of 2 Company,
2nd Go Mon Battalion of the
Quyet Thang Regiment. Vanh was
awarded the American Killer Hero
medal for his role in the March
2nd ambush.
*Photo courtesy of
Nguyen Dinh Thang*

Nguyen Van Phi
intelligence officer for the
Quyet Thang Regiment, later
wounded and taken prisoner by
the Americans before joining the
ARVN forces to fight his former
Viet Cong comrades.
Photo by the author.

Nguyen Ngoc Nham
As 34-year-old lieutenant he
commanded 1 Company 2nd Go
Mon Battalion of the independent
regiment Quyet Thang
"Determined to Win." A native of
Ben Tre province in the Mekong
Delta his military career began as
a 16-year old Viet Minh guerrilla
fighting the French. By March 2,
1968 Nham had also undergone
10 years of training in North
Vietnamese military schools.
Photo by the author.

Nguyen Van Phi points to the spot
where he discovered several of the
dead members of Charlie Company
while doing his battle damage
assessment after the ambush.
The bodies were recovered by
the Manchus on the morning of
March 3.
Photo by the author.

Epilogue

"What good is it going to do to talk to some poor woman about a husband who died so long ago," John Henchman asked me when he learned I was planning to talk to the family members of those who died.

I, for one, do not want focus put back on this—no matter your interest in making this a story to show the bravery, or whatever, of the Manchus. No matter your skill, you will not overcome the perception that somebody, or several somebodies, screwed up.

If you want to portray a gallant battalion at its best, there are many more operations that would qualify. Besides the Hour Glass, there is Bo Tuc on December 20, when we defeated a full regiment or more of NVA, and one of

our own was recommended for the Medal of
Honor — a young lad who kept firing his
machine gun until his fires were masked, and
then he continued to fight with his bayonet
and an entrenching tool until he was killed in
his hole. That is the stuff of legend. Check out
Bo Tuc in the Recollections. True, you were
not there for these two very important
battles, but you came to the battalion after
Hoc Mon, too. Why not focus your energies
on showing us at our best? I have no doubt
there are tons of guys who could fill you in on
all the details of both of these, and you could
weave a wonderful story around either.

Henchman's response to my request to talk about the
March 2nd ambush was one that bothered me a great
deal as I set about researching the ambush of Charlie
Company, especially his point that digging into this
story was bound to bring back awful memories and
cause pain. I wasn't sure I had a good answer for why I
was doing it. Nothing I was attempting could change
anything, and maybe it wouldn't make any difference
so many years later, maybe it really would serve no
useful purpose. The only motivation that seemed to
make sense was my feeling that maybe my own reasons
for trying to find out what happened and why would
be shared by others. That hunch had been reinforced
in conversations with others who served with the
Manchus in Vietnam. Thanks to the Internet, we had

begun to find each other after having gone our separate ways for more than thirty years.

It started when Bob "Willy" Dixson, one of the men who with the Manchus when they first arrived in Vietnam in 1966, started a Web site, "Willy's Place" (http://www.oregoncoast.com/willy/). The Web site was a collection of photos he had taken in 1966 when he served with Alpha Company of the Manchus and again thirty years later when he returned to Vietnam on a visit. The Web site became a magnet, and soon a guest-book list of visitors became a roster of men who had served with the Fourth Battalion, Ninth Infantry during its four-and-a-half years in Vietnam. Within a short time, the list had grown to the point that a reunion was organized, and for the first time in three decades, the Manchus were able to make good on the promises they had made to each other to stay in touch.

But as good as it was for many, there were also those who avoided the reunions. They had gone on with their lives and did not want to dwell on the past. "Let those poor dead boys rest in peace," was how former Charlie Company commander Willie Gore put it when I asked for his help in putting together their story. "Nothing good can come of it," he said. When I explained that my intention was not to find fault or place blame but rather to show what those men went through, he said it couldn't be done. "Only those who were there will ever know what it's like," he said. "Words can't do it." After all the years that had passed he felt nothing good could come of telling the story of the ambush. Not surprisingly perhaps, given the greater amount of time he spent with the First Air Cavalry, the unit he was assigned to after recovering from the wounds he suffered in the ambush, he said he felt a greater connection to them than to the Manchus.

Gore had spent the remainder of his tour—nearly ten months—with the Seventh Regiment of the First Air Cavalry Division, where he also commanded a company. Despite the findings that lack of flank security was the cause of the ambush and the finding that Gore was to blame for it, his career did not suffer. He retired after twenty-nine years at the rank of colonel.

It is also not surprising that there were others there that day who declined to talk about what happened. Few American soldiers, even those who served with the Manchus, had experiences anything like Charlie Company had on March 2, 1968. Even though the Manchus were a line-infantry battalion that saw, collectively, much action over the four-and-a-half years they were deployed in Vietnam, not everyone had experienced combat at the same level of intensity. So it was no surprise when the men who had lived through the ambush seemed reluctant to attend the reunions. When they did come, or when they began joining in the public dialogue on their own e-mail mailing list, they were reluctant to talk much about the bad things.

More than once, more than one man expressed the

sentiment that the Manchus' experience in Vietnam should not be summed up by the March 2nd ambush. The battalion had had many successes, and it would be wrong to dwell on this one incident, which could make it seem as though they had failed as soldiers. But there were also those who said that to ignore it would be a disservice to those who died that day, that it would be wrong to leave the impression that their deaths could have been preventable but for the incompetence of their leaders. Some said not talking about what befell Charlie Company would play into the hands of those who wanted to keep a lid on the event, who thought it better to portray the event as a colossal military blunder by a low-ranking officer and let it go at that than to admit that on one day on a road outside Saigon the Viet Cong carried out a masterfully planned and executed ambush. We were supposed to be winning the war, so it was better, by this reasoning, to leave the impression that only gross incompetence could lead to such a loss.

Many of the Manchus who contributed to this book feel deep sorrow that John Henchman has borne the responsibility and, perhaps, most of the guilt for what happened. They consider him one of the best commanders they ever had. He and his operations officer, Bill Roush, were respected and held in high esteem. Many in the battalion considered Roush to be the spiritual leader of the Manchus. One officer in the battalion said of him, "We thought he was invincible." Another went so far as to say, "If Roush had been alive on March 2nd that ambush would never have happened." The praise the Manchus have for Roush and Henchman is as real as the genuine care and concern both leaders had for the men in their command. As one Manchu put it, Henchman not only knew the names of the 400 men in his battalion, he knew their nicknames, too.

If I had been apprehensive about how the American survivors would react to my probing into the ambush, I had no idea how I'd be received, or even if I'd be received, when my research took me back to Vietnam. Would I get government permission to do this kind of historical research? Even if it were granted, was it just wishful thinking to believe that I would manage to find our former enemies. But my motivation to find out their side of the story, in addition to getting a comprehensive look at the ambush, was strong.

Something more than 60 percent of the population of Vietnam is under the age of thirty. For them the American War, as they call it in their history books, is just that: history. For an American veteran of that war, going to Vietnam really puts things in perspective and slays lots of dragons at the same time. When we, the guys who fought there, say the word *Vietnam*, we are talking about more than just a place. It connects to too many old memories that many of us wish we didn't have. But quite a bit of what an American soldier remembers when he says the word *Vietnam* does not exist anymore. In fact, I'd say most of it doesn't. Yes, there is still this small Southeast Asian country named

Vietnam, but that's about the extent of the similarity to what is in our memories. Being there proves the war is really over.

I sent off an initial query to the press office of the foreign ministry, asking if it might be possible to visit Vietnam to conduct some research. In a matter of just a few weeks, I got a positive answer and instructions about whom to contact to make arrangements for my work.

But disappointment soon set in, and for a while it looked like I was going to get nowhere. The foreign-ministry official I was told I was to check in with in Ho Chi Minh City, as Saigon is now called, did not answer any of my messages, and I was unable to make contact before the narrow window of opportunity stipulated in my visa opened. I had no choice but to go and hope the official would be more receptive when I pitched up on his door step.

I called the official the first morning of my stay and got a very cool reception. He did not seem happy to get my call. First, he said he was busy and couldn't see me at all. But after pleading my case and explaining that I had been calling and sending e-mails for more than two weeks without receiving any response from him, he reluctantly agreed to a meeting. Evidently his softened heart hardened in the intervening six hours, for when we met face to face, he pointed out officiously that his office had no budget for helping people like me with projects like mine and that I would have to pay all the expenses associated with a trip to the ambush site. I told him not to worry and promised to cover all the expenses, even before I did the quick mental calculations and figured out that it couldn't cost that much to rent a car for the twenty-mile round trip to the ambush site.

Seeing that I wasn't put off by that particular obstacle, it was clear the official would have to find another. So, he called in a colleague for consultations on the matter. He introduced me to Number 2, my "project officer."

I sat quietly while the office air conditioner hummed and the two foreign ministry officials rattled away in the curious singsong staccato of the Vietnamese language. After what seemed like quite some time, the official informed me that it was out of his hands, and he could do nothing for me.

"At all?" I asked.

"You see Phu Long is not in the Ho Chi Minh district. It doesn't belong to me," he said.

"But I don't want to go to Phu Long. My business is in Hoc Mon district," I interjected, knowing full well that in the first go-around he had recklessly mumbled in English, "Ah, that area"—a pudgy finger smudging my new map—"belongs to Ho Chi Minh City."

"Yes, of course," he frowned, waiting for the next insurmountable problem to occur to him. "But I never received any written instructions from Hanoi, so you see it is completely out of my hands."

"Perhaps I should contact the foreign ministry in Hanoi," I offered.

"Yes, of course," he said. "But these things take time.

And then there is the matter of budget."

I said I understood, reminded him that I had agreed to pay whatever expenses might be incurred, thanked him for his time, and said I would contact the foreign ministry in Hanoi, which could perhaps pass along the approval that had been given to me along with my visa.

"Is that map made in Vietnam?" he asked as I stood to leave.

"No, it's American."

"Good. We can use it," he said folding it carefully and handing it to Number 2.

During the short trip down the stairs of the foreign-ministry building and out to my waiting rental car and driver, I consoled myself with the thought that I had had the foresight to order two maps of the Hoc Mon area from the U.S. Geological Survey. When I got in, I saw my driver had that copy draped over the steering wheel and had already puzzled out how to get to Hoc Mon and route 248, the scene of the ambush.

I stopped off at the hotel and sent off a brief e-mail to Hanoi asking for my contact there to be kind enough to inform my foreign-ministry contact in Ho Chi Minh City of my plans and to ask for his help. Then, with fingers crossed and a prayer that a miracle would break the bureaucratic log jam, I was on the road to Hoc Mon. All the while I was poking around the Hoc Mon area, trying to reconcile the memories of the area I had gotten from the ambush survivors with the way the area looks today, I was thinking it was going to be "one of those days." But when I got back to my room that night an e-mail from Hanoi was waiting, telling me that my Ho Chi Minh foreign ministry contact had been briefed and was now ready to help. I got through to him and he confirmed that he now had the go-ahead from Hanoi and would begin getting in touch with the local officials so that all the necessary permissions will be in order. I then decided to give him a little time.

Telling the story of the physical layout of the ambush site required piecing official documentation together with the recollections of those who had been there. Some of the recollections were quite detailed; others less so. None of them matched completely. Fortunately, the official record of the event, while quite sketchy in many respects, did provide a picture of the place, especially if one takes the time to piece together the descriptions that are in the interviews the division historian conducted in the few days immediately after the event.

Even without official permission to conduct the sort of research I need, I had already made several trips to the ambush site in order to get a solid orientation. This was my fourth trip to try to get a feel for the landscape. I had spent time in the immediate vicinity in June 1968, when I had been platoon leader for the Third Platoon of Delta Company of the Manchus. I had also visited during a trip in 2000. The place has changed a lot in the past thirty-six years and is nearly unrecognizable from the perspective of how it looked the day of the ambush. There are now houses, shops, post offices, and other buildings along both sides of the road, where before there had been only rice paddies and orchards. But there were still some landmarks.

I needed to be able to verify the exact spot of the ambush. I checked the coordinates that fellow Manchu veteran Larry Mitchell had found in copies of the battalion operations log and compared them with accounts given by survivors immediately after the ambush. Then I had to marry that information with details I had gotten in interviews in recent months. There were some minor discrepancies, but in the end they all matched. The bridge first identified by Bob Dixson in 1998 was indeed the bridge that marked the point at which the Go Mon ambushers cut off the rest of the battalion from coming to help Charlie Company. Anybody on the south side of that bridge was in the killing zone of the ambush. Anybody on the north side came under withering fire from Viet Cong positions in the north-facing banks of the canal.

There could be no doubt. I had found the place. The bridge does look different from the pictures taken the day of the ambush, mainly because it is a new structure that sits higher above the road surface than the original it replaced. The supports for the old bridge are still visible, however. I was not so lucky when it came to finding the ARVN compound that had been south of the ambush site. John Henchman had radioed the American advisor to that group, asking for help, but he never got it, neither did he get an explanation for why.

Interviews with locals revealed that the old ARVN compound buildings were used as a small military base when the new government took power in 1975, but it was soon found to be inadequate and was torn down. The exact area is known as Ap Nam Thang, which is part of the Hoc Mon district. During the first visits, I avoided speaking to anyone except to say hello and smile. I didn't want to have my visa curtailed and get sent home for some perceived violation of the terms of my entry in the country. By the time I got permission and began my interviews, I had visited often and taken many pictures. My activities were not unnoticed, but my intent was clearly misunderstood. I had assumed that locals would have taken one look at a foreigner of my age wandering through their villages and would have assumed I was just another one of those former G.I.s who had come back searching for his lost youth. The truth was revealing. Since almost everyone in those villages is new to the area and most were born long after the war ended, their thoughts didn't turn in that direction at all. They saw me taking pictures of bridges and thought I must be some engineer. A few had gotten excited about the prospect of civic improvements and were visibly let down when they learned what I was up to.

As I began trying to nail down the exact site of the ambush, I applied the grid coordinates from the operations logs to my new map from the Defense Mapping Agency. It was a perfect match. However, the map (published in 1979) did not have the detail I would have preferred; it did not show, for example, what I found out by driving the road. Between the northern outskirts of Saigon and the point where highway 248 swings west, for example, there are five bridges more than any of the earlier information indicated. One of them spans the Ben Cat canal, which is about 150 yards wide. Another goes across the Saigon River.

Through a process of elimination, I whittled them down until I was left with three bridges that "could" have been the location that marked the northern end of the killing zone. When I found two of those bridges only a few hundred meters apart, I knew I was nearly there. The men from the other companies who had tried to come to Charlie's aid spoke of an uncontested bridge they had had to cross before reaching the bridge that marked the boundary of the ambush. The more southerly of these two bridges had to be it, the northern boundary of the ambush. That bridge spanned the body of water that had separated Charlie and Delta Companies. It was the bridge where Denny Dubendorf and Leroy Williams had taken refuge from the three Viet Cong soldiers of Lieutenant Nham's First Company had tried for more than seven hours to kill them.

My biggest hope was to encounter some Vietnamese who had been there. They might have many answers to the questions that the Charlie Company survivors had been asking themselves for all those years. Maybe they could even explain to me why the soldiers in the ARVN compound never came to help. There were still blanks in the story. If only I could find some Viet Cong

who had been there. Perhaps it was too much to hope
for. Even if I did find them, would they be willing to
talk? Despite the opening up that Vietnam has been
undertaking in the past decade or so, it remains a very
closed society, with tight governmental controls. People
might not be too willing to talk. That thought was
reinforced when my driver, a former South Vietnamese
soldier who had endured several years in a re-education
camp run by the North Vietnamese victors, was visibly
nervous as we drove through the area.

"Beaucoup VC," he said using a phrase I had not
heard in thirty-six years. "Lots of VC. Be careful."

As we traveled the area I was reminded again of the
huge tidal fluctuation in the canals. They almost dry
out at low tide and fill up until they are at least six- to
eight-feet deep at high water. Even the very large Ben
Cat canal dries out significantly, leaving a very narrow
channel on the southern side of it that is still navigable
by the shallow draft boats that use it. Even those boats
draw no more than about three feet, so we're not
talking a lot of water at low tide.

Pictures taken at high and low water show the
huge fluctuation. The native sons of the Quyet Thang
Regiment, the Otters, would have been well aware
of the tides and would have always taken them into
consideration when planning their operations. It
clearly made a huge difference to those guys in Delta
Company who were trying to cross the canal and came
to Charlie Company's aid. It was just one factor but an
important one and helps to illustrate just how well the

ambush had been planned.

As I scoured the area, I took pictures of landmarks I thought some of the survivors might recognize. I forwarded several photos to them to see if they could identify anything.

One of the pictures I had great hopes for was of a gravestone just off the west side of the road at about the point where Dan McKinney had lain wounded. Dan had told me of seeing a Viet Cong soldier peering out from behind a tombstone, and I was hopeful I had found it. Dan couldn't recognize the tombstone. The one he remembered had been a single stone and not part of a group. Whether or not the other stones now at the site were new additions and that made it look different, it didn't look right to Dan, so I was out of luck.

I had much better luck, at least initially, when John Henchman said, Yes, he could confirm that the small stone building in a picture I had sent had indeed been his Battalion Command Post (CP) the night before the ambush. The location was potentially important since the CP location had been a serious point of contention between Henchman and the brigade commander, Raymond Miller had ordered Henchman to clear out of the building, saying it was a Buddhist shrine. Henchman had believed it to be simply a house with a small shrine in the living room, not a religious site. In the end Henchman disobeyed the order to leave and gave his command group at least one night of relative luxury after the very long, fatiguing, and emotionally wrenching days of the Hoc Mon operation.

If this was the place, it was where the colonel had been coordinating with his artillery liaison officer when the ambush was sprung. Henchman had run out to the road to try to see what was going on but hadn't been able to see much, only the approach to one of the bridges and some Manchus down on the road. I paced off the distance and estimated it to be approximately 300 yards to the small building that was the battalion CP, just as the grid coordinates from the battalion journal said. It made sense.

But as I described the building and its location further Henchman began to have doubts, so I was left unable to say with certainty that it was the building where the Manchu commander had set up his headquarters for the night. I did learn that the building Henchman had at first thought was his CP was, in fact, the Chua Thien Linh (Heavenly God) Buddhist Pagoda. Built in 1958, it had been abandoned following the Tet Offensive at the end of January, 1968 and was, like most of the other houses in the area, not re-occupied until October of that year. Another day of disappointment.

Finally, the foreign-ministry man in Ho Chi Minh City cleared me to begin my interviews. So, with my government-approved translator, I set off in search of some Viet Cong.

Almost directly across the street from the Heavenly God Pagoda is the home of Mrs. Tran Thi Mui, sixty-five, who has lived there continuously since 1960. She was not able to shed much light on what had happened the day of the ambush, as she and most of the other local residents had fled a month earlier, when the Tet Offensive began. Similar stories were recounted by other old time residents. Eighty-six-year-old Tran Van Nhanh said the intensity of the fighting in the area made it almost impossible for them to stay. No one I spoke to knew of any former Viet Cong still in the area. Most, they said, had died in the war. Nguyen Van Het said he would have been a Viet Cong fighter, but the wounds he suffered when his Viet Minh commando squad was ambushed by the French in 1954 at the nearby Phu Long Bridge over the Saigon River had left him crippled and unable to run.

Trung Van Meo, sixty-five, who had been a driver in the South Vietnamese Army, told me he knew of one Viet Cong commander still living nearby. He had told me the same story when I had met him during my first trip back to the area in 2000. But I had not been able to follow up on his tip at that time. Now, four years later, he had some bad news for me. Mr. Meo and the half-dozen other people I spoke to seemed to believe that the Viet Cong who had carried out the ambush were not local. I was told that a local group of Viet Cong, some 200 men, had been wiped out in a major fight with the Americans. I knew that a mechanized unit of the Twenty-fifth Division, Third Squadron of the Fourth Cavalry had fought a pitched battle in the Hoc Mon area about the time Mr. Meo was referring to. The details of that battle, known as the 3/4 Cav battle, were a little better known, at least in U.S.

records, and it did not seem to correspond with what
the Vietnamese civilians were telling me. The 3/4 Cav
battle had been fought near a bridge, but it had taken
place on a highway some ten kilometers to the west.

Still, there was one more question mark I had
to erase. To do that I would have to find someone
who had been there and who remembered what had
happened on March 2, 1968. I began to wonder. If the
Vietnamese I had been speaking to were correct, then
the local Viet Cong group might have been destroyed,
and the Viet Cong who had fought the Manchus on
March 2 were not local at all.

I had always heard, and almost every Manchu I
interviewed believed, that the men that had carried out
the ambush were from the Go Mon battalion. There
are a few references to that unit on veteran Web sites,
in particular to a small suicide squad from the Fourth
Go Mon that is said to have taken part in the attack on
the ARVN military headquarters during the first day
of the Tet Offensive. None of the locals I spoke to were
familiar with the name Go Mon, although Mr. Meo,
the former ARVN, pointed out that the it derives from
a combination of the name of the town of Go Vap and
the nearby district of Hoc Mon. For a brief time after
the war the Hoc Mon district had been renamed Go
Mon in some sort of communist gerrymandering, but
the name change did not last long and the two districts
were never permanently merged into one. So maybe
there had been a Go Mon battalion, in fact several
battalions of them, after all. If so, then it would have

had soldiers drawn from an area much broader than the immediate vicinity of the ambush in the Hoc Mon District. That was both good and bad news. Good, in that the fact that I hadn't found any former Viet Cong near the ambush site didn't mean that I wouldn't find them elsewhere. The bad news was that "elsewhere" could cover a lot of ground and make for a much larger haystack to find the needles in.

I found the first one the very next day.

The search that day began like every other day I spent in the area. I pulled up at a house I had not already visited and asked if anyone in the household had lived there in 1968 and remembered a big battle there in March of that year. As usual, I was greeted with a polite, "No, we moved here in 1992." But this particular morning, the man we had asked said, "Wait. The man across the street, he should know. He's been here a long time."

Optimism slightly renewed, I headed across the road to the restaurant the man had pointed to, only to have our hopes dashed when a man who looked to be in his mid- to late thirties greeted us. "Oh no," he said. "I wasn't even born then." He paused, and just as I was thinking it was time to move on, he said, "But my father would remember. He was a soldier with the liberation forces here then."

"Where can I find your father," I asked.

"He's right over there, having coffee," he said, pointing to the darkened interior of the restaurant. "I'll go get him."

Nguyen Van Phi spends much of his time at the small restaurant he and his son run at the intersection of the two main roads just north of the ambush site. It is the spot where the big Chinook helicopter flew in the afternoon of March 2 with the three-quarter ton truck slung under it on a cargo strap , the truck used to pick up the dead Manchus. He is the former intelligence officer who served with the Second Go Mon Battalion of the Quyet Thang Regiment.

Nguyen Phi had been there the day that Charlie Company was ambushed. I wanted him to confirm to me that he was talking about the same incident and that he hadn't gotten it confused with something else like the big fight with the 3/4 Cav in February of 1968. He said, no, he was sure, it was the time they killed all those Americans just a little ways down the road. I asked if he could take me there. He said he could. So we got into my car. I asked him to tell the driver where to go. He told the driver to turn around and head south. Then, with no prompting from me, he told the driver to stop. We got out, and he gestured to the spot on the side of the road where he had crawled up to get an assessment of how bad the damage was. It was no more than one hundred yards south of the bridge and canal, the exact spot where some of the dead had lain.

Phi also was able to confirm to me that the Quyet Thang Regiment was made up of three Go Mon battalions. He said the Go Mon were better known to the locals by their nickname of the Otters. Each battalion had included three companies of thirty to forty fighters each. Most had been young men, but some had been boys, and there had even been five or six girls who had fought alongside him. What the Manchus knew to be the Go Mon Battalion was actually one of several battalions in a regiment.

There is a curious twist to Nguyen Phi's story. Late in 1968 he had himself been caught in an ambush, this time planned and carried out by Americans. He had been wounded and taken prisoner. After he recovered from his wounds, he had been given the chance to serve with the South Vietnamese Army. Strange as it may seem for someone who had fought at least four years against the Saigon government and its U.S. allies, he had accepted the offer and served the remainder of the war as an ARVN soldier. While serving with the South Vietnamese forces, he was severely wounded a second time, in a major 1969 battle in Long Binh, and saw no more fighting for the duration of the conflict. He now lives with his wife, two sons, and quite a few dogs in his combination restaurant and home less than a half a mile from the March 2nd ambush site.

Before I left I asked Nguyen Phi what he would say if he had the chance to meet with some of the American soldiers. He answered rather quickly, "The days of those life and death issues are past. It is time to forget them. I have no bad feelings for the Americans." I explained that what I meant was what would he say to the survivors of the Charlie Company ambush? "I would wish them good health," he said. "And for their families, too. We must cherish life and peace. We are lucky to be here. We are lucky to be alive."

As I got up to leave he pressed a picture into my hand. It was a passport-size photo of him taken when he had been a Viet Cong fighter in 1968.

During our time together Phi had explained that the Go Mon battalions were a mixed group of Viet Cong and NVA and that they had, in fact, been formed that way. NVA officers had moved into the area as early as 1965 to recruit, train, and equip a Viet Cong force. One of the men sent from Hanoi to do that was Nguyen Dinh Vanh. He served as deputy commander of one of the companies in the Second Go Mon Battalion.

"Do you know where I can find Mr. Vanh," I asked.

"Yes," Phi said. "He died last Friday."

Disappointed, I headed off to find the house where Vanh had lived, hoping family members might be willing to tell me about their relative and his part in the ambush. It didn't seem likely, but it was worth a try. I did meet with his family and learned some of what happened from the tales he had told his son, twenty-six-year-old Nguyen Dinh Khanh, a currently serving officer in the People's Army of Vietnam. Mr. Khanh said his father had been recognized as a great hero as a result of the March 2nd ambush. He was also one of twelve survivors of the Go Mon Battalions, which had been surrounded and destroyed just a few days after their great success.

"But if you really want to know what happened in the ambush," Khanh's mother Truong Thi Kim Lien said, "you should talk to the historian of 2 Battalion."

"There is a historian who has written about the battalion and the ambush," she said. "Do you want his phone number?"

After having met with the intelligence officer of the Second Go Mon battalion, I thought I was prepared for where my research might lead. I was not. Nguyen Phi had been at the ambush but had served only as an observer to help spot and identify the location of Charlie Company. Nguyen Ngoc Nham had been the commander of First Company, Second Go Mon Battalion and had taken an active role in the ambush.

When we met Nham was seventy years old and possessed a detailed memory of the ambush, which is aided by the history he has written of the battalion.

He greeted me in the back garden of his upscale two-story home in Go Vap, which is now a section of Ho Chi Minh City. He walked me in through the kitchen, apologizing for the mess, as his wife was busy cleaning up after breakfast. We sat in the dining room at a large and expensive-looking hardwood table. Laid out on the table were cups for tea and a book, *The History of Quyet Thang - 2nd Battalion Go Mon*. It was opened to the section where he had chronicled the events of the March 2nd ambush.

Over the course of the next four hours, he provided me a detailed account of the ambush from his point of view as a company commander. Not everything he told me was easy to hear. He came across as self-confident, bordering on arrogant. He jokingly referred to his experiences in a way that made it seem he felt his years of fighting were a lark. He sipped his "333" beer and smiled as he bragged of his exploits.

"I would kill an American with one hand and turn around to make tea with the other," he said more than once.

Nham said that in the beginning he had worried what it would be like to fight the Americans with their helicopter gunships and jet fighters and bombers. And he admitted that before his first fire-fight with the Americans, he was apprehensive about the physical differences between his small, thin fighters and the larger, more powerful looking G.I.s. But in the end he concluded that the American soldiers themselves would not have been much of a concern were it not for the powerful air support they had had at their beck and call. He felt he had had a clear advantage when he faced the Americans, whose tactics were, to him, unsound. They rarely used cover and concealment, their movements were plodding, and they were slow to react when attacked. His body language suggested something approaching contempt when he said those same criticisms applied not only to the tactics employed by U.S. forces but also to the individual American soldiers he faced on the battlefield.

"We were always quicker to react than the Americans," he said. "We could fire off a whole magazine at an American before he got his weapon pointed in the right direction. They were really no good as soldiers."

By the time of the March 2nd ambush, Nham, then thirty-four, had spent almost half his life as a soldier. He had begun fighting the French as a Viet Minh guerrilla in 1950, at the age of sixteen. After the French defeat at Dien Bien Phu, Nham had wanted to return to his home town in the Delta, but his commanders singled him out for further training and sent him to Hanoi where he began serious military training. It was during that time that he began to show promise as a shooter. By 1965, when he was ordered to go south to train an insurgent force, he was an expert marksman who would have as part of his mission the job of training the guerrillas he would help recruit in the fine art of the sniper. The Manchus came to appreciate how well he did his job, for the Go Mon fighters were renowned for their marksmanship and for how often their victims were shot in the head.

Nham explained. Most times, it was the only body part the sniper could see, so that is what he shot at. Given a choice, he explained, his men would shoot at the torso, or "center of mass," as he put it. Had he himself been a sniper? "Oh yes," he said. Did he know for sure if he had killed any Americans?

"Twenty-one," Nham answered.

"I was given the American Killer Hero medal," he added, "our highest award."

The day Charlie Company was ambushed is one he remembers with great pride. His soldiers had carried out their instructions flawlessly. His company had only lost one man, one of his platoon leaders, 2d. Lt. Nguyen Van Chieu, who was shot by an American carrying an AR15. Was he sure it was an AR15, not the similar M-16? Indeed he was, he answered, and proceeded to draw an accurate sketch of the weapon on a scrap of paper he pulled from my notebook.

"We never found Lieutenant Chieu's body," Nham said. "He is still MIA."

If the two Go Mon Battalions that carried out the ambush suffered few casualties that day, their luck was not so good just days later. The First and Second Battalions were caught out in the open, away from their otter dens in the Red Beetle Military Zone. Trapped on one side by the Saigon River and the other by an American blocking force, they were slaughtered by sortie after sortie of cobra gunships. Of the more than 200 Viet Cong guerrillas in the two battalions, all but twelve were killed. Nham was himself seriously wounded in the incident. He underwent surgery in an underground clinic and was then carried to Cambodia, where he spent two years recovering from the wounds to his chest, stomach, and right leg.

After the war ended, Nham spent a dozen years working for the Veterans Department of the People's Republic of Vietnam. Despite his stature as a victorious liberator and war hero[36] he found his career going nowhere. Suspecting his lack of advancement was northern prejudice against a southerner he turned increasingly bitter and took early retirement in 1986.

---

36. Nham received the American Killer Hero medal for his actions in the March 2nd ambush.

He was given a plot of land in Go Vap, the once small village that is now an indistinguishable part of Ho Chi Minh City. He applied for a home loan that he was qualified to receive as a veteran but never got it. So he built the home himself in stages, as he could afford it.

"Damn government," he snorted.

As we finished our interview, I asked Nham if he thought about the war much. I got no answer. When I asked what he thought of me—a former enemy and a symbol of the nation he had fought for so long—he threw his arm around my shoulders and said we had a lot in common and that maybe we could even become friends. Then he told me that for him the war was over and that he had put all that behind him. There is nothing to be gained by dwelling on the friends and family lost, he said.

When I asked if he ever had any thoughts about the men whose lives he had taken, especially the men of Charlie Company of the Manchus and the ambush he remembered so well, he said simply,

"It was war. They were the enemy. I tried to kill as many as I could."

THE DEAD

JOSE LUIS ALVAREZ-TAPIA

GERALD LAWRENCE AVERY

CHARLES EDWARD BONDS

HARLAN RAY BRANDTS

JERRY WALTER BYERS

WILLIAM BRACE CAWLEY, JR.

ALVIN LLOYD CAYSON

NICHOLAS JOSEPH CUTINHA

BRUCE ELIOT, JR

GARY VIRGIL FRAZIER

MICHAEL DENNIS FROST

RAYMOND LEROY GALLAGHER

CAL DUAIN JOHNSON

LAWRENCE JOHNSON

JACK JOSEPH JORDAN, JR.

LEE ROY LANIER

CHARLIE FRANK LEE

JAMES RUFUS MATHIS

ROBERT JUNIOR MC GEE

CHARLES EDWARD MELOTT

LEONARD DAVID MOORE

THOMAS LEE MORK

BARRY LEE MOYER

JAMES FRANCIS O'LAUGHLIN

KENNETH LINDLE OLDHAM

WILLIAM RASSANO

JOSE ANGEL REYES

ROY DONALD PAGE

RONALD LANDON SALVANI

WILLARD SKAGGS, JR

MICHAEL ROSS RIVERS

ARISTIDES SOSA

CLIFFORD GEOFFREY STOCKTON

RONALD ALLEN SLANE

WARREN LEE TALL

JOHN MICHAEL THOMPSON

DANNY GEORGE SWAZICK

WALTER C VELVET, JR.

LARRY HUSTON WALDEN

CARREL JEAN TITSWORTH

PAUL EDWARD WEST

DARRELL EUGENE WHEELER

GARY WINSTON WATKINS

JOSEPH JEROME WILLIAMS

VIRGIL LAWRENCE WILLIAMS

LARRY ALLEN WIDENER

DANNY STEPHEN YOUNG

WILLARD FRANK YOUNG

KENNETH WAYNE WINGET

THE WOUNDED

PFC FLORENCIO ALVAREZ
PFC LENNY C. ALIMENIOUS
PFC JAMES C. ELLIOTT
SP4C JOHN J. GALLIGAN
PFC. ERNEST C. GOOCH
CAPT WILLIE L. GORE
SGT. DONALD K. GUTHRE
PFC. CURTIS W. JONES
PFC RUDOLPH LOVE
PFC AUGUSTINE LUGO
SSGT. JESSE B. LUNSFORD
SP4C DANNY LUSTER
SP4C.CHARLES MCCAMISH
PFC. DANIEL L. MCKINNEY
PFC ROBERT W. PRESTON
PFC. KENNETH R. PIZER
PFC. WILLIAM R. POCKHUS
PFC. LARRY A. REDITT
SP4C. LEONARD ROYSTON
SP4C. ELSWORTH RUNION JR.
PFC. MARTIN K. SHOEMAKER
SP4C. JAMES S. SWANTEC
SP4C. CONLEY A. TILLSON
IST LT. FRANKLIN R. TINKLE
SGT. DONALD W. WHIPP

SP4C. LAWRENCE W. WILSON
PFC. BOYLE
(A/SIXTY-FIFTH ENGINEERS)
SP4C. SULLIVAN
(A/SIXTY-FIFTH ENGINEERS)

INDEX

U

V

W

Y

ABOUT THE AUTHOR

L. D. James was an infantry platoon leader in Vietnam. He has been a news editor and reporter for The Associated Press and Agence France Press and was a regular contributor to Time magazine and National Public Radio. For more than fifteen years he reported for the Voice of America from more than 50 countries in Europe, Africa, the Middle East and Asia. He has covered wars and civil wars in Liberia, Rwanda, Bosnia, Macedonia, the Gulf War, Afghanistan and the Iraq War. He lives in Washington, DC with his wife Sonja.